HERE'S HOW TO GET THE MOST OUT OF YOUR COPY OF *SMART RETIREMENT*:

Throughout this book, we've provided a number of interactive websites. These sites were designed to help you understand key concepts, and a member of the SMART Advisor Network has made them available to you. Access these important online resources with the following six-digit SMART Access Code:

_____

For tax-aware retirement income planning:
www.TaxSmart4Life.com

For debt elimination and lifelong freedom from debt:
www.DebtFree4Life.com

To see the effect of annual market returns on your savings:
www.SecureIncome4Life.com

PRAISE FOR *SMART RETIREMENT*

"I believe that many tax professionals will think differently and advise their clients differently after learning about the Strategic Movement Around Retirement Taxation®. The concept of tax-aware planning and the diversification of taxable distribution sources in retirement is really straightforward but not well understood. I've just never seen it described anywhere else better than here in the *SMART Retirement* book."

—STEVE MAGNONE, CPA

"I've read a lot of textbooks on taxation while getting my masters in tax, yet this is the book that contains the most actionable and useful information about postretirement income taxation for a retiree and those approaching retirement. It's incredible to have this valuable tool available to help my clients understand how the Strategic Movement Around Retirement Taxation® increases the value of their money in retirement and enhances their income, wealth, and legacy at a time when Congress has changed the law to end the stretch IRA and now is looking to eliminate the step-up in basis on capital gains."

—ZACH HESSELBAUM, ESQ., LLM

"Matt, you have done it again! Your previous work has enhanced the lives of countless Americans, and no doubt this will too. Being in an industry that seems to have forgotten that without clients, we are all out of a job, it's a comfort to know there are some people who really do care and share information that can have a positive impact both now and for future generations.

As you read in *SMART Retirement* about what the 'big boys' are doing with their money, you might think, 'Yeah, but look at how many millions they have.' What this book teaches us is that although the 'big boys' may have more zeroes in their account balances, the principles around debt elimination and tax-aware planning are the same for all of us. I hope this book does for you what it has done for me and my clients."

—RON CAMPBELL, CFP, CAMPBELL FINANCIAL SERVICES

"Once you understand the three dates that completely altered the face and future of the American retirement system, you immediately know that old-world ideas are not going to solve these new-world problems. SMART is the solution that creates a true private reserve wealth strategy for my clients."

—TOM BORIS, ESQ., ELDER LAW OFFICES OF SHIELDS & BORIS

"For me, SMART's value is truly found in the attention it gives to the preservation of family wealth. I'm a family-oriented person, and modern financial planning has turned a blind eye to the preservation of principal—something that was ingrained in my thinking and beliefs growing up in western Pennsylvania. I believe you shouldn't spend what you've saved; instead, you should live off the interest your savings earn and get debt-free as soon as possible. SMART has that same effect but with better economics, lower effective tax costs, and lower effective interest rates, all while offering a plan for these low-yield times. SMART is more than a strategy; it's a shift in how lawyers, advisors, and tax professionals need to think when representing their clients. I highly recommend this book."

—JIM SHIELDS, ESQ., ELDER LAW OFFICES OF SHIELDS & BORIS

"For the past fifteen years, our firm has consistently looked to Matt Zagula to help with the design and development of outstanding client solutions by combining financial products with innovative trust designs to minimize our client's effective tax costs. Throughout our long relationship, Matt has shown himself to be a man of vision and integrity. His latest book on the Strategic Movement Around Retirement Taxation®

is a must-read for anyone over the age of thirty. This is especially true today, with tax policies and the political climate making it a must to have a plan for the strategic movement around rising taxation."

—RICK L. LAW, SENIOR PARTNER AT LAW HESSELBAUM; AN ESTATE, ASSET PRO-TECTION AND RETIREMENT INCOME TAX LAW FIRM

"I've spent my entire career in the financial services and insurance industry so the concept of actuarial arbitrage really resonated with me. Once I understood the value in the 'math' of SMART, compared to normal Wall Street and banker math, I became a true believer in SMART. Do yourself a favor—get SMART and learn the truth about money and how to break free from lifetime indebtedness and excessive taxation."

—SCOTT LUSTER, INSURANCE EXECUTIVE

"I love this book. After more than thirty years in the financial services industry, it's great to read something truly innovative. This book gives real hardworking people the tools they need to design a SMART strategy with their savings by taking advantage of techniques that the financial elite has been using for years! SMART does not offer a traditional view of financial planning, but once you learn what America's wealthiest individuals and their families are doing with their money, it only makes sense to be SMART about your own retirement planning."

—NANCY BRUNETTI, OCEAN CREST FINANCIAL

SMART
RETIREMENT

FOREWORD BY **DR. MICHAEL F. ROIZEN**

FOUR-TIME *NEW YORK TIMES* #1 BEST SELLER

SMART

RETIREMENT

DISCOVER THE

STRATEGIC MOVEMENT AROUND

RETIREMENT TAXATION®

MATT ZAGULA

ForbesBooks

Published by ForbesBooks, Charleston, South Carolina.
Member of Advantage Media Group.

ForbesBooks is a registered trademark, and the ForbesBooks colophon is a trademark of Forbes Media, LLC.

Printed in the United States of America.

10 9 8 7 6 5 4 3 2

ISBN: 978-1-950863-82-2
LCCN: 2021905266

Cover design by George Stevens.

This publication is designed to provide accurate and authoritative information in regard to the subject matter covered. It is sold with the understanding that the publisher is not engaged in rendering legal, accounting, or other professional services. If legal advice or other expert assistance is required, the services of a competent professional person should be sought.

Advantage Media Group is proud to be a part of the Tree Neutral® program. Tree Neutral offsets the number of trees consumed in the production and printing of this book by taking proactive steps such as planting trees in direct proportion to the number of trees used to print books. To learn more about Tree Neutral, please visit **www.treeneutral.com.**

Since 1917, the Forbes mission has remained constant. Global Champions of Entrepreneurial Capitalism. ForbesBooks exists to further that aim by bringing the Stories, Passion, and Knowledge of top thought leaders to the forefront. ForbesBooks brings you The Best in Business. To be considered for publication, please visit **www.forbesbooks.com.**

TABLE OF CONTENTS

THE WORLD IS CHANGING. ARE YOU?

Two of Three Important Dates

How Taxes Adjust

Taxes and Cash-Flow Pressure

That Third Date and Why the Market May Not Save Us

The Trouble with RMDs

THE TRUTH ABOUT THE "FUZZY" FINANCIAL MATH BANKS AND WALL STREET USE

Revealing the True Cost (And Consequence) of Debt

The Rate of Return Myth

Planning Your Descent: More Important Than the Climb

USING BASIS AND FLOAT TO GAIN FINANCIAL FREEDOM

It's Smart To Know Your Basis

The Benefits of Tax Awareness and Actuarial Arbitrage

GET SMART: ENJOY THE STRATEGIC MOVEMENT AROUND RETIREMENT TAXATION®

From the SMART Whys to the SMART Hows

Where Should You Invest Your Money?

The Moral of the Story

SMART PEOPLE, SMART PLANS

Higher Income without Taxation

Understanding Where Am I AT™

MY PERSONAL SMART PLAN

The Negative Side of Life Insurance

How Carriers Make High Cash Value Life Insurance

How To Create Six Figure Annual Tax Deductions With Pension Plans

How I Used Research & Development Tax Credits

To Eliminate Taxes Dollar for Dollar

Why Banks Match My Retirement Savings With

$3 of Their Money to $1 of Mine

IS IT YOUR TIME TO GET SMART? I HOPE SO. HERE'S WHY.

Time To Get Smart?

Disclosure and Acknowledgment

FOREWORD

I know it is unusual for a medical doctor to write a foreword to a financial book. After all, doctors are known as traditionally bad financial managers. But I know how intertwined your financial well-being is to your health. After all, I've authored or coauthored four number one *New York Times* best sellers on aging, each of which describe how important managing financial stress is to your health (yes, we all have financial stress, no matter how much money we have), as well as coauthoring with Jean Chatzky of NBC Today the recent *New York Times* best seller, *AgeProof: Living Longer Without Running Out of Money or Breaking a Hip.*

The unusualness of a doctor writing a foreword on a financial book should underscore for you, the reader, just how unusual this book is. The SMART Retirement system is eye-opening in its approach, enviable in its lucidity, and awesome in delivering action-able information. Now, a medical doctor is rarely, if ever, that enthusiastic about a book or anything financial, even when it involves maneuvers that help you maximize your after-tax income decades from now.

So what is different about this book? Well, first, no financial advisor has ever focused my attention so clearly on the net or after-tax income I will receive after retirement. No advisor or planner has ever told me about how the government has laws that teach me the way they want me to receive those monies. And until now, no financial advisor has told me of these connections and pathways to more spendable income in retirement the way that Matt Zagula does in this book. That clarity and those insights, ending with actionable steps, is what makes it, in strictly nonmedical terms, awesome.

The healthiest body in the world won't stay that way if you're frazzled, with about six figures worth of debt, or worried about whether your retirement funds will fund your lifestyle. (I dislike using the word retirement, as I think you will always stay active but rather just change your focus on what activity you want to pursue and why you pursue it. But for this foreword, I'll use retirement to indicate that period of time after you stop the job you had that led to accumulating money.)

When I started reading this book, I realized this was a bright, eye-opening approach. It wasn't about how to accumulate dollars (spend less, save more, I know) but about how to position that money to have the maximum amount to spend every year in retirement and still leave a legacy. It focused my attention so clearly on the after-tax income I will receive, which seems so obvious a goal I began to wonder why no one else had ever mentioned it to me.

SMART Retirement isn't just about accumulating money, something that Matt likens to climbing up the mountain, which is hard enough. It is really about how to maximize what you have to spend from that hard step of accumulation—so that the difficulty in accumulating can be worth the effort, and the trip down the mountain can be rich, fun, and all you dreamed it could be. Although Matt doesn't promise it, following his methods, you will be able to do more of what you dreamed of doing.

You see, what's different about this book is that it isn't about how to invest in any one type of investment to maximize that accumulation. No, instead Matt takes you through a SMART Retirement process that provides you with a systematic approach to getting what you want and need out of your retirement so that you can be comfortable and less taxed. He then helps you compound these tax-advantaged dollars, using straightforward math, to leave a meaning-ful legacy—money that your surviving spouse, children, and grand-children will need. In Matt's words, "SMART will guide you in the Strategic Movement Around Retirement Taxation®, teaching you how to take advantage of tax and actuarial opportunities."

Matt presents these opportunities with a crispness and clearness that even a doctor can understand. He shows you how to do this the way the big companies do when they provide for their CEO's retirement, not with a 401(k) or stock options but with what the US government wants you to do. Yes, the government wants you to own a home—that's why it made mortgage interest deductible on your taxes. And the US government wants you to delay Social Security withdrawal—that's why it increases the amount you receive about 8 percent per year after age sixty-two. But I didn't realize the gov-ernment wants me to own a cash-value-building, low-death-benefit life insurance policy and Roth IRA till I read it here. And that the government makes it tax-advantaged to access the funds in both the Roth and the policy after it is paid up.

The reason a SMART Retirement plan is important—right now—is that the world is in the middle of a pretty large shift when it comes to aging. How old do you think you'll get to be? Seventy-seven? Eighty-four? Ninety-two? One hundred? Whatever number popped into your head, chances are that you're about as wrong as a steady diet of junk food. You're going to live longer than whatever number you picked (even longer than preservative-filled junk foods, some of which can last in your refrigerator for years, by the way). Just consider this: In the past three decades, life expectancy in the

United States has jumped for men from seventy to seventy-nine and for women from seventy-seven to eighty-three.

Over the last hundred or so years, one innovation after another has prolonged life: the tuberculosis vaccine (1921), penicillin (1929), high blood pressure meds (1947), the surgeon general's warning on cigarettes (1969), seat belt laws (1984), tests for inflammation becoming routine (1986), vaccines for preventing cervical and throat cancer (2004), and for treating a specific cancer (2006). With so many life-threatening problems not needing as much attention, medicine can focus on managing chronic conditions such as arthritis, asthma, diabetes, or osteoporosis. Even some types of cancer and HIV/AIDS are now considered manageable. The result? Life goes on longer than ever before, with you being able to live younger no matter what your age. It's like cars now lasting two hundred thousand miles on average, compared to sixty thousand miles in 1970.

While the change in longevity should be exciting, the truth is that longevity comes with a price. Because we're living longer, it's more expensive to fund retirement. That's true even if you're in good shape. Surveys from financial institutions note that running out of money before running out of time is by far our biggest financial fear. One survey even found that running short of funds is a bigger fear than death. Going the distance means we all need a new set of skills, new strategies, and a new way of thinking to have that money. And, as Matt Zagula keeps pointing out, it isn't just that you saved enough but that you put it in the right vehicles at the right time to maximize the amount of money that your savings provides you to live on "after taxes."

This book is about giving you the power to take the ride of your life for the second part of your life—all without limping around with duct tape over your rear bumper. Matt Zagula is clear and generous with his knowledge. He even suggests books to read after this one. He presents a plan to thrive financially through that second part of life.

When you read this book, you'll see that Matt gives you the needed pieces and the knowledge to solve the puzzle of retirement planning and tax arbitrage. Matt makes the strategies clear, with well-defined action steps. Plus the book is fun to read, and that is saying a lot for a financial planning book. In the end, having enough money to last is romantic, which means this book may even improve your love life—and that's good for your health too.

MICHAEL F. ROIZEN, MD

Chief Wellness Officer (CWO)
Roizen Family Chair, the Wellness Institute of the Cleveland Clinic

ABOUT THIS BOOK

The world can be a scary place these days. A lot has changed. Yet, despite the changes in our world, economy, and political atmosphere, recommendations from traditional financial planners and the investment advising community have pretty much stayed the same. When the market is down, we still hear the endless refrain of "Hold on, it'll come back." When the market is up, we're consistently told that we should "buy into this strength."

This book is dedicated to questioning the financial sense of believing we can continue to solve new-world problems with the same old answers. I'll take a very firm position and tell you that we cannot do that—continually recycle old ideas—and expect to be successful with them. Instead, I want to offer you, the much-appreciated reader of this book, insight into a different way to view your planning as you build toward retirement. For those of you who are already in retirement, I'll encourage you to focus on what really matters ... the money that comes to you each month *after* your taxes are paid.

The SMART Retirement planning process, which stands for the Strategic Movement Around Retirement Taxation®, is a system I developed so that my clients, and the clients of other SMART Advisor Network members, can remain focused on their primary goal of achieving the greatest net after-tax retirement income without cannibalizing their principal.

In these low-interest-rate, yield-strapped times, the financial planning and advisory community are quick to throw in the towel on their clients' end-of-life principal balances in favor of what has been popularized as safe money advising or income planning. These are red-flag terms that translate into: *We will use your assets to promise you a lifetime income but guarantee nothing for the preservation of your principal for your family after you die.*

Years ago, I worked as a consultant for companies that promoted these types of plans to advisors. What I found was that their marketing pitches were parallel to an airline's preflight instruction. You know the one—"In the unlikely event of a loss of cabin pressure, panels above your seat will open revealing oxygen masks. Reach up and pull a mask toward you. Secure your own mask first before helping others." In much the same way, these companies seemed to be telling their clients not to worry about their families, their legacy, or the security of their capital ... just their income!

Soon this became the slogan of the income-planning, safe-money marketers who promoted these ideas and concepts to advisors desperately searching for yield for their clients. Eventually, many started to believe it was acceptable to just focus on income through-out retirement—which alone is not enough. As you'll later learn, even reputable research firms, such as Morningstar, are now finding that the safe withdrawal rate from your retirement funds is equal to just 2.8 percent per year—and the way they define safe is simply making sure you don't completely run out of money before you run out of life. No joke!

In their January 21, 2013, study, "Low Bond Yields and Safe Portfolio Withdrawal Rates," Morningstar makes it clear that their definition of success is *not running completely out of money in retirement.* It's shocking to believe that based on their findings, if you take just $28,000 per year from a $1 million IRA with 40 percent of its holdings in stock, you have a 90 percent chance of not going broke (account value to $0).[1] Again, keep in mind, success in this example means not going broke. It doesn't mean keeping $1,000,000 of principal; it simply means not going to $0! Weird definition of success, isn't it?

You might think that reducing your risk and shifting assets from stocks to bonds could possibly solve this income problem, but that doesn't seem to be the case. Morningstar's expert research team found that if you drop the stock market exposure on a $1 million IRA from 40 percent to 20 percent, it actually reduces the distribution rate from 2.8 percent to 2.7 percent. Of course, this also means that doubling your stock market exposure adds only a paltry one-tenth of 1 percent to your potential retirement income distributions. It makes you wonder if that's worth the risk.

It's hard to justify, at least in my conservative mind, accepting this level of risk for only $27,000 to $28,000 per year from a $1 million IRA before taxes. And let's say you're like millions of Americans who don't have $1 million saved. Let's say you're sitting on a $100,000 retirement account balance. That gives you just $2,700 to $2,800 per year—again, before taxes!

All of this information is probably making you question whether you can achieve an attractive retirement income with the money you have saved. You may even be asking yourself if it's reasonable to believe you can acquire enough from now until retirement to achieve a reasonable postretirement lifestyle. The challenges presented by this prolonged low-yield environment paved the way for the rise of the income-planning niche within the financial advisory and

---

1   David Blanchett, Michael Finke, and Wade Pfau, "Low Bond Yields and Safe Portfolio Withdrawal Rates," Morningstar, January 21, 2013.

planning industry. These planners offered a solution with their ironically named safe-money strategies. I'd agree it solved the low-yield dilemma, but at what cost? Their client's principal—maybe a portion of it or maybe all of it, depending on how long their client lived and the market conditions during their retirement.

I believe the safe-money, income-planning crew missed a few very important realities. One of the biggest things they missed is the fact that the oxygen mask we put on ourselves first must also be passed on to the people we love most. Every single day I look at my teenage son Charlie, whom I love, admire, and am so proud of, and I cringe, knowing that the economic future he faces is not an easy one. I think about these facts:

- The days of defined benefit plans, when a company provided monthly pension income upon retirement from service, are gone!

- Today younger workers rely mostly on their 401(k) plans. You'll learn as we progress through this book that 401(k) plans provide a very useful tool for the accumulation of money but are poor vehicles for the distribution of that money once we reach retirement. I'll show you exactly why this is and how to start fixing these issues now, even if you are already in retirement! The 401(k) is like chocolate cake—a piece is delicious, but if you go and eat the whole thing, you'll end up miserable.

- It is our responsibility to learn and then expose how banks and brokerage firms use fuzzy math to "help" us fund our present and plan our future (and, yes, the sarcasm here is intended). The banks take advantage of us and perpetuate America's amortization illiteracy, and it's our job to become informed and take back control. As you read, you'll learn the right way to calculate interest on loans, how misleading the concept of average rate of return is when your goal is retirement income, and why your rate of return in retirement is, at best, a half-truth. You'll learn for yourself that *when* you earn money is much more important than *what* you earn in retirement.

• Social Security is admittedly cooked. Visit their website and see for yourself. The year 2020 will be the first year since 1982 that Social Security's cost is expected to exceed its income and interest. Worse, sometime around 2035, the system becomes insolvent, which is just a nice word for financially broke, not shocking when you consider it's a system that is broken. But don't take it from me, take it directly from the Social Security website, www.ssa.gov:

Social Security's total cost is projected to exceed its total income (including interest) in 2020 for the first time since 1982, and to remain higher throughout the remainder of the projection period. Social Security's cost will be financed with a combination of non-interest income, interest income, and net redemptions of trust fund asset reserves from the General Fund of the Treasury until 2035 when the OASDI reserves will become depleted. Thereafter, scheduled tax income is projected to be sufficient to pay about three-quarters of scheduled benefits through the end of the projection period in 2093. The ratio of reserves to one year's projected cost (the combined trust fund ratio) peaked in 2008, generally declined through 2018, and is expected to decline steadily until the trust fund reserves are depleted in 2035.[2]

---

2   "A Summary of the 2019 Annual Reports," Social Security Administration, www.ssa.gov/oact/ trsum/.

My goal is for the SMART Retirement planning process to empower you to look past the marketing and advertising slogans and half-truths being thrown at us every day, funded by the big advertising dollars paid by America's wealthiest banks and Wall Street. I hope to guide you to ultimately put your family's oxygen mask on without endangering your own financial breath and to ensure that your post-retirement phase is as comfortable as you expected it to be while you were saving money in preretirement.

So what is the SMART Retirement planning process? First, it's a systematic approach to getting what you want and need out of your retirement so that you can be comfortable and less taxed. It then goes on to help you compound these additional tax-advantaged dollars, using straightforward math, to leave a meaningful legacy—money that your surviving spouse, children, and grandchildren will need.

SMART will guide you in the Strategic Movement Around Retirement Taxation®, teaching you how to take advantage of tax and actuarially enhanced opportunities. These opportunities will become clearer as you read through the material.

Ultimately, you'll be introduced to one of the ways our country's most successful and celebrated investor, Warren Buffett, continues to compound wealth within his holding company, Berkshire Hathaway, by effectively understanding the profit potential of *actuarial float*. Float has been such a significant wealth-building warehouse for Buffett that he specifically uses the term forty-six times in his 2015 letter to shareholders of Berkshire Hathaway.

If Buffett has such enthusiasm for this actuarially enhanced and tax-advantaged opportunity, I would imagine those of us who are motivated by getting the most out of our hard-earned money would too. I'd think we'd be willing to take the time to learn how to use a version of this powerful concept within our own personal finances.

At the end of the day, we all want to secure a better financial future for ourselves and our families. That's what SMART is ultimately about. It's not a secret scheme to get rich quick or a hyped-up, shady tax loophole. It's about good old-fashioned smart planning, with modest portions of your accumulated wealth, for a tricky new economic outlook.

If you're ready to invest the time to think a little outside the old financial planning and asset management box, to study, and to get SMART, then you're ready to learn how to profitably integrate the Strategic Movement Around Retirement Taxation® into your overall financial plan.

ACKNOWLEDGMENTS

I want to take this opportunity to acknowledge the significant contribution a few individuals have made to the world of finance. Often, hindsight is 20/20 and I believe many will look back and realize their retirement could have been better if they had been exposed to these two gifted thought leaders and authors.

First, I want to recognize Nelson Nash, the creator of the Infinite Banking Concept and author of *Becoming Your Own Banker*. Nelson was a self-taught Austrian economist who went beyond the theory of money, economy, and national wealth and literally brought it to your kitchen table. His book should be mandatory reading starting in the eighth grade and required each and every year thereafter. With his Infinite Banking Concept, you never really graduate, you just get better as time goes on. It is, without any hesitation, one of the best books on personal finance ever written. You should read it as soon as you finish this book. Mr. Nash has passed away since this book was first written, but his brilliance continues on through his teachings. Thanks, Nelson. You will be missed by many who learned from you.

Next, I'd highly recommend you read Barry James Dyke's book Guaranteed Income: A Risk-Free Guide to Retirement. Barry is one of the finest financial researchers you'd ever have the privilege to learn from. It speaks volumes that the former US comptroller general, David M. Walker, wrote the foreword to Barry's book. I give a copy of Barry's book to every single one of my new clients as they go through my SMART Retirement planning process. With so much misinformation out there both online and offline (through the media, which serves their advertisers and their own financial interests), Barry's book brings the truth, proves it, and then reveals what the SMART money people actually do with their wealth. It's an eye-opener when you see what financial industry CEOs do with their own wealth compared to what their companies do when they offer to manage yours. I'll refer to Barry's research a number of times in this book, but that's no substitute for reading Guaranteed Income.

I'm blessed to work with a large number of extremely talented financial professionals and CPAs. These professionals now realize the importance of recapitalizing the retirement wealth lost to their clients' income needs in these low-yield times, so that wealth can be passed on to support their spouses and the next generation. We are fortunate to have passionate advisors, like Nancy Brunetti, who was the first SMART Advisor Network member and is consistently generous with her time and resources as she mentors others on the SMART ways. These professionals help make the SMART Advisor Network what it is today. They continue to amaze me as they grow in their knowledge of bringing a tax-aware approach to building wealth, distributing income, and implementing a total wealth-management process for their clients in a more tax-diversified way.

I am equally blessed to work with some of the most successful multidisciplinary law firms in America. These talented counselors not only navigate the complexities of trust law, estate planning, income tax, and estate tax laws for their clients, but they also understand how to synergistically weave suitable financial products into their clients' plans, enhancing the benefits of the trusts they create and making financial products work better at the lowest possible effective tax cost while also working more efficiently toward the clients' goals than would otherwise be possible with the financial product alone.

A special thanks and acknowledgement also goes to Brad Barlow, SMART Planz CEO and chief actuary. Brad is a true math wizard and 401(k) and cash-balance pension plan design expert. I'd also like to thank leading pension and fiduciary lawyer Rob D'Anniballe Jr. of Pietragallo, Gordon, Alfano, Bosick & Raspanti. Rob has been instrumental in the development of the SMART techniques. And to Paul McManus, a SMART marketer who serves many SMART Advisor Network members by communicating the SMART message through social media and other education-based mediums.

I also want to thank and acknowledge my hardworking team at SMART Retirement. These conscientious, client-first-focused professionals are the backbone of my organization. A huge thank-you to my partner Pam Weaver, and our wonderful team: Debbie Shay, Daneen Cline, Aaron Gurskey, Lesli Yingling, and our case design and planning specialist, Ryan Driscoll. Thanks also to my friend and SMART advisor mentor, Tracey Spikes, who puts in incredible time and energy working with the network members to deflect the effect of debt and taxes. A huge thanks to Tom Gober, the forensic accountant at The SMART Advisor Network. As America's top fraud expert to trial lawyers and law enforcement agencies nationwide, Tom was that critical addition we needed to always protect our clients from misplacing their trust with substandard companies. Finally, I'd like to thank my book editors who I kept busy.

Lastly, I'd like to thank my mother and father who encouraged me to challenge conventional wisdom and think differently while always putting first the best interests of those I serve and represent.

CHAPTER 1

THE WORLD IS CHANGING. ARE YOU?

It will likely come as no shock to hear me say that the world is changing. Look at our debt, our national and international politics, and the economies of all the great nations around the world. It's a crazy time filled with unprecedented problems, innovative but largely untested solutions, and general insecurity about what the future brings.

If there's one thing we know, it's that we can't fix new-world problems with old-world solutions. That would be like trying to treat cancer with a combination of leeches and snake oil. We have to adapt and find alternatives. We need progressive solutions that factor in all the changes surrounding us while helping to insulate our money and our future from what will come ... whether good or bad. But first, we need to understand the truth about what's going on.

Here is the truth that we need to face: In recent years, there have been three dates that changed the face and future of the American retirement system. Because of these dates, it doesn't matter which political party controls what branch of the government. Our financial future is in trouble. Although all the politicians today want to make it about the vote—telling you that if you vote for their candidate, this-and-that is going to get better, that it's so-and-so's fault for absolutely everything that's wrong—the reality is that these three dates I'll mention are what really changed the face of America's financial future.

No matter what person holds which office, these dates, and their impact on the future, cannot be changed by any politician. They're just facts that will affect our lives and the financial future and security of our loves ones.

TWO OF THREE IMPORTANT DATES

The first financial-future-changing date was **January 1, 2008**. It was on this day that the first baby boomer turned sixty-two years old and qualified to take early Social Security distributions. Now, if it was just one baby boomer, that would've been fine—but it wasn't. In fact, this date was the turning point, often referred to as the "silver tsunami," when the seventy-six million baby boomers born between 1946 and 1964 would begin to hit sixty-two and, as such, qualify for early Social Security distributions.

January 1, 2008, was just the first wave in our silver tsunami, because on **January 1, 2011**, the second of our three important dates, the first baby boomer turned sixty-five. At that point, they not only qualified for higher Social Security benefits than at age sixty-two but, if they weren't still working at a company that offered health insurance and they were retired, also had a new primary healthcare provider: Medicare. And guess what? Every day after that date we've had an average of ten thousand baby boomers turning sixty-five and qualifying for the same benefits. Imagine that—twenty thousand new potential Social Security and ten thousand new potential Medicare recipients every single day.[3] Never before have we had such a large, seemingly unending stream of people ready to tap into retirement and healthcare programs all at one time.

So what does this do to our country? Look at figure 1. I think it tells a very important story. This graph represents the percentage of the US government debt to the entire gross domestic product (GDP) of our country. This is all of the economic activity that goes on and what percentage of that economic activity represents our government debt.

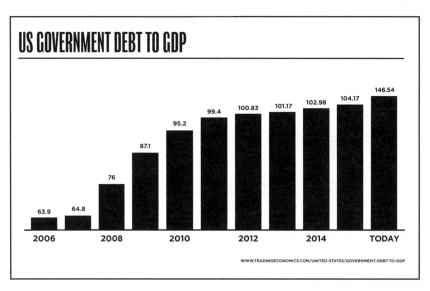

Fig. 1

Notice the comparatively small numbers in 2006 and 2007 and then the conspicuous spike in 2008. In 2008, when those first baby boomers had the opportunity to take Social Security, well …

---

3   "Baby Boomers Retire," Pew Research Center, December 29, 2010, http://www.pewresearch.org/daily-number/baby-boomers-retire/.

some of them did—and it spiked our ratio of debt to GDP. That's what you see reflected in that graph. The next year, more eligible baby boomers signed up to receive their promised benefit. Of course, by 2010 even more did. In 2011 we see a more sustainable upward trend as Medicare costs rise over time in much the same way health insurance would.

The change we see in the ratio between government debt and GDP right as baby boomers started relying on Social Security is a primary factor underlying my belief that taxes must be adjusted significantly upward over the long haul. The current tax law sunsets on December 31, 2025, so we know that taxes are definitely going up on January 1, 2026. When they do, I believe they'll go higher than the previous rates and way up over the long term. The current administration has a perfect setup in the House and Senate to make immediate changes. I suspect we will see a number of adjustments to capital gains, step-up, and various rate changes, including to payroll taxes. While we may see lower tax rates now, but ultimately the country's debts must be paid—and that means taxes must rise. I believe that traditional planning is failing because it is not willing to acknowledge and adapt to this financial reality, likely due to regulatory limitations imposed on advisors and the advice they are permitted to provide.

HOW TAXES ADJUST

Taxes adjust in one of two ways, if not both. The first is through increased tax rates. This is where the government tax authority says, "Hey, the rate was 15 percent; now it's 20." As mentioned, rate increases are something that will occur on January 1, 2026, after current tax rates expire on December 31, 2025.

The second way taxes are increased is through what I call *rollbacks*. Let's just imagine a service right now that's paid for by Medicare. Next year, Medicare says, "Instead of paying providers directly, we're going to reimburse you, and we're going to pay less for that service." When Medicare pays less, a retiree's supplemental insurance has to make up the difference. I can tell you, though, that insurance companies aren't going to offer this coverage out of the kindness of their hearts. During the next year, when that supplemental insurance incurs this added cost, the expense has to be reimbursed and paid back to the insurance company in the form of higher premiums *paid by the senior who's supposed to be receiving these promised benefits.*

So when I say taxes are going up, and they have the potential to go *way* up, it's because I believe that the percentage rate of taxation will increase significantly. I also believe that promises that were made will be rolled back or potentially even reneged on.

In my area of the country—the Rust Belt where there's a lot of manufacturing—we know that pension plans and health insurance, what were commonly referred to as *legacy costs,* put many local companies out of business. Unlike the government, these companies actually did put money aside to meet their obligations to their employees. The companies then discovered, painfully, that it was really hard to keep up with the healthcare costs and income distribution obligations of their promised pension plans when people started taking money out from their pension funds.

Our government, saddled with a lot more retirees than at any time in our nation's past, has the same financial burden—but it's a lot worse. Unlike business owners, the government never put any money aside. The more people who call in and say, "Hey, these are the promises you made and we want to collect on them," the more money our government has to either print or tax to get. Ultimately, this results in higher taxation.

This isn't a problem that can be solved politically. This is an age demographic issue, and make no mistake about it, our population is aging. Back in the 1950s, there were sixteen workers for every one Social Security recipient. That allowed us to spread the responsibility over a wide number of workers so they didn't really feel the pinch, and the government could fulfill its promises. Today, our population is aging, and in 2015 we fell to a three-to-one ratio—which meant we had only three workers for every one Social Security recipient that year.[4] In 2019, that number dropped to 2.8. So every year, the workers feel the pinch a heck of a lot more.

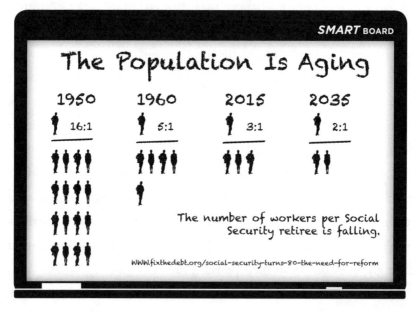

Fig. 2

How long will the government be able to sustain this? It appears it can for another fifteen years or so. We know this by looking at the Social Security website, where they clearly disclose that there is a point when the government says the Social Security system simply

---

4   "The Growing Class of Americans Who Pay No Federal Income Taxes," Tax Foundation, https://taxfoundation.org/growing-class-americans-who-pay-no-federal-income-taxes/

doesn't work anymore—that it's broken. That time comes in 2035, when reserves are depleted and we have close to two workers paying for each Social Security recipient. And there is no political solution to this. This is an age demographic issue and an economic issue. It's just undeniable. Again, here's what they have to say about it:

Social Security's total cost is projected to exceed its total income (including interest) in 2020 for the first time since 1982, and to remain higher throughout the remainder of the projection period. Social Security's cost will be financed with a combination of non-interest income, interest income, and net redemptions of trust fund asset reserves from the General Fund of the Treasury until 2035 when the OASDI reserves will become depleted. Thereafter, scheduled tax income is projected to be sufficient to pay about three-quarters of scheduled benefits through the end of the projection period in 2093. The ratio of reserves to one year's projected cost (the combined trust fund ratio) peaked in 2008, generally declined through 2018, and is expected to decline steadily until the trust fund reserves are depleted in 2035.[5]

Just as we see a falling number of workers paying the benefits for each Social Security recipient, we also see fewer people paying taxes. Here's a sobering fact for you: Of the 157 million people working in America, there are approximately only thirty-five million who earn enough to file a tax return with tax due. Add to this the reality that 169 million Americans receive some form of money or services paid for by the government, and you've got a reason to be concerned.

That disparity contributes greatly to an imbalance of revenue and on the amount of interest paid per citizen on our existing national debt. Today the per-citizen tax revenue is $10,460 and the interest paid on our $27,871,793,000,000+ debt and unfunded Medicare and Medicaid liabilities is $14,969. When you delve further and look

---

5   "A SUMMARY OF THE 2019 ANNUAL REPORTS," Social Security Administration, www.ssa.gov/oact/trsum/.

at the debt per citizen ($84,170) versus debt per taxpayer ($222,191), you can clearly see that the burden on tax-paying Americans is getting exponentially worse.

So what happens when the tax revenue is insufficient to pay the government's interest payouts? Higher taxes! But not for everyone. In fact, the people hit hardest are those professionals who are "high-earning not rich yet." These HENRYs are shouldering the burden of our shortfall, and it's only going to get worse as we see things like long-term capital gains tax rates and step-ups in basis disappear. Income taxation alone is no longer sufficient to manage the national debt, let alone reduce it. Please check the facts for yourself at www. USdebtclock.org.

TAXES AND CASH-FLOW PRESSURE

Taxes *can* go up. Even though most people feel like taxes can't get any worse, we've seen them much worse in the past. And the wealthy will be disproportionately affected by the increase, as you can clearly see when just 35 million taxpayers (of the 157 million who file) make a payment to the IRS. What does that almost punitive tax structure do to the motivation levels of the wealthy? Well, let's take a look at former president Ronald Reagan to get an idea.

Reagan was the highest-paid movie actor in the early 1940s. If you look at figure 3, you'll see that at that time, the top marginal tax bracket over $200,000 was 88 percent.[6] If you add in California's state tax, it's said that Reagan was paying over 91 percent in taxes, which meant he had little incentive to make more than two movies a year. In fact, he is quoted as rhetorically asking former Secretary of the Treasury Donald T. Regan what good it would have done him to have filmed a third picture each year. Instead, he would do two

---

6   Henry Blodget, "The Truth About Taxes: Here's How High Today's Rates Really Are," *Business Insider*, July 12, 2011. http://www.businessinsider.com/history-of-tax-rates.

movies and then he was done because most of the money he earned above that would have been lost to taxation. So he had no incentive to keep going to the set and making movies and instead chose to "loaf" six months of the year.[7]

A TAX POLICY SET BY PERSONAL EXPERIENCE

US FEDERAL MARGINAL TOP AND BOTTOM TAX RATES - 1913-2015

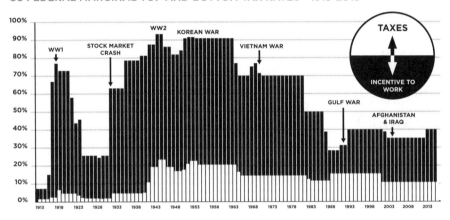

Fig. 3

Many believe that Reagan's was one of the greatest economic minds ever to preside over this nation. I would argue that his tax policy seems to have been set primarily by his individual experience. Just take a look at the US federal top marginal and bottom marginal tax bracket from the inception of taxes back in 1913 and you can plainly see that taxes have been much higher than they are now.

As Reagan's example already proved, the higher taxes go, the less incentive people have to work—and the incentive to work is very important because many of the benefits that were promised to seniors are going to be paid for *by younger workers' payroll taxes*. We

---

7   Gerald Strober and Deborah Hart Strober, *Reagan: The Man and His Presidency* (Houghton Mifflin, 1998).

can't completely disincentivize them from working, especially since there are only three paying for every one Social Security recipient. But we risk doing just that because we need to raise taxes and likely roll back promised benefits to eventually manage our nation's ever-expanding debt.

So we are in a very unique economic time. Once again, the world has changed, and it's not like any single politician or party can fix it and bring it back to some fiscal normalcy that we understood in the past. It's a new situation, and income taxation is not enough. Asset taxation is the new focus, as we saw in 2019 when the SECURE Act was introduced.

THAT THIRD DATE AND WHY THE MARKET MAY NOT SAVE US

One of the things that always comes up when I'm meeting with a client is what my thoughts are on the market—and boy, has it been good for a while now. It's at this point that I let clients know that I don't manage people's money. As I'll explain later, I focus my firm on tax recharacterization and debt elimination, rather than on fee-based money management.

That said, there was a time when I felt that inflation would make the market go up because things just naturally get more expensive over time. But today, I think there's a different and more likely scenario going on. My new response is that I think the market is under significant **cash-flow pressure**, and that cash-flow pressure is going to worsen over time. Here's why:

Remember those three dates we talked about? We've already talked about 2008 and 2011. Now let's talk about the third date, **July 2, 2016**. On that date, we finally felt the peak of the silver tsunami hit our shores, because the very first baby boomer hit age

70.5 and, under the old rules, began taking required minimum distributions (RMDs) from certain tax-deferred retirement plans, including the Traditional IRA and 401(k) plans. Every single day of the three years since, we've had roughly ten thousand baby boomers turn 70.5 years old. Let's talk about the market consequences of aging baby boomers taking those *required* distributions. Under current law (the SECURE Act), required distributions now begin at age seventy-two—but for how long? The senate has reintroduced an alternative to the SECURE Act that pushes the RMD age to seventy-five. Sounds good in theory, **BUT** it also requires a five-year settlement for your nonspousal beneficiaries after your death. That means your kids will be forced to pay taxes on inherited IRA funds that much sooner. As always, beware of "tax breaks" from a government that **needs** your money!

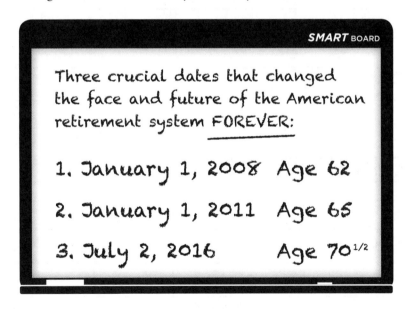

Fig. 4

THE TROUBLE WITH RMDS

When you have a tax-deferred retirement account, like a Traditional IRA, you defer paying taxes on the contributions you make over the years. You also grow your money—again, without taxation. The IRS doesn't let that go on forever, however, so at age seventy-two (as of 2020), they require pretax plan participants to begin taking taxable distributions based on their age, life expectancy, and balance from the prior year. The IRS has a uniform table that tells seniors how much they must take. I've published their table here.

REQUIRED MINIMUM DISTRIBUTION Table effective until 2021

Table III (Uniform Lifetime)

Age	Distribution Period	Age	Distribution Period	Age	Distribution Period	Age	Distribution Period
72	25.6	84	15.5	96	8.1	108	3.7
73	24.7	85	14.8	97	7.6	109	3.4
74	23.8	86	14.1	98	7.1	110	3.1
75	22.9	87	13.4	99	6.7	111	2.9
76	22.0	88	12.7	100	6.3	112	2.6
77	21.2	89	12.0	101	5.9	113	2.4
78	20.3	90	11.4	102	5.5	114	2.1
79	19.5	91	10.8	103	5.2	115 and over	1.9
80	18.7	92	10.2	104	4.9		
81	17.9	93	9.6	105	4.5		

Once you determine a separate required minimum distribution from each of your traditional IRAs, you can total these minimum amounts and take them from any one or more of your traditional IRAs.

REQUIRED MINIMUM DISTRIBUTION New 2021 table

Age	Distribution Period	Age	Distribution Period	Age	Distribution Period	Age	Distribution Period	Age	Distribution Period
72	27.3	84	16.8	96	8.3	108	3.9	120 +	2
73	26.4	85	16	97	7.8	109	3.7		
74	25.5	86	15.2	98	7.3	110	3.5		
75	24.6	87	14.4	99	6.8	111	3.4		
76	23.7	88	13.6	100	6.4	112	3.2		
77	22.8	89	12.9	101	5.9	113	3.1		
78	21.9	90	12.1	102	5.6	114	3		
79	21	91	11.4	103	5.2	115	2.9		
80	20.2	92	10.8	104	4.9	116	2.8		
81	19.3	93	10.1	105	4.6	117	2.7		

Fig. 5

Essentially, the way RMDs work is you take the account balance from December 31 of the prior year and you divide it by the number in the Distribution Period column next to your age. Some people ask me what this number means. It's a joint life expectancy, assuming that your spouse is ten years younger. They call it a uniform table because that's what everybody uses even if you are unmarried, widowed, or married to an older spouse.

Let's convert this into an example to make it easier to understand. In our example, we have Mary, a retiree who is seventy years old. In a couple of years, Mary will reach age seventy-two and have $100,000 in her IRA. During that year, she must start taking minimum distributions, so according to figure 5, she must take the balance of her IRA and divide it by 27.3. That means that her distribution would be $3,663.

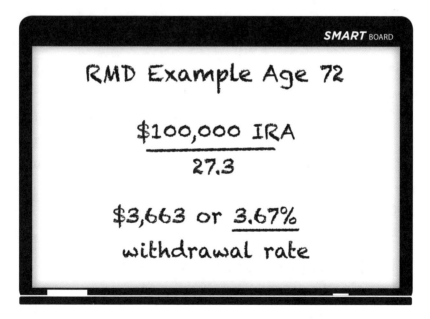

Fig. 6

Let's reverse this and consider what percentage of her overall balance that distribution represents. In this case, the required distribution of $3,663 divided by $100,000 is 3.67 percent. That seems pretty low, right? It's less than 4 percent, which is what many traditional retirement planners suggest for withdrawals, so maybe the IRS is onto something with their formula!

Or … not—because according to the information provided by Morningstar, a leading investment research firm in North America, 3.67 percent is a very large and possibly unsustainable distribution rate in today's low-yield environment.

Now maybe some of you have heard of Morningstar, the publishers of the report shown in figure 7. Their accurate, insightful, unbiased reports are used by countless brokerage firms, planners, asset management firms, and others. In 2013 they published a study of their findings on low yields and safe withdrawal rates from retirement plans. The authors of the study were notable and accomplished PhDs with advanced degrees in economics and finance. They concluded that our ability to avoid running out of money in retirement was based on taking no more than 2.8 percent a year from our accounts over a thirty-year retirement.[8]

Just think about that: 2.8 percent. On a $100,000 account for our retiree, Mary, that would be $2,800—quite a difference from the $3,663 the IRS will require Mary to take. In fact, it's over 30 percent more than what Morningstar's experts consider "safe" if the goal is to be highly certain you won't run out of money in retirement.

LOW BOND YIELDS AND SAFE PORTFOLIO WITHDRAWAL RATES

January 21, 2013

M⌀RNINGSTAR®

Fig. 7

---

8   Blanchett, Finke, and Pfau, "Low Bond Yields," Morningstar.

Here is the withdrawal grid that describes the safe withdrawal rate based on retirement period and asset allocation. This grid from the Morningstar study defines your probability of success based on your account **not going to zero**. Success, in this report, does not mean that your basis (your principal, the invested capital) in your account is preserved for your loved ones, but that your account will not run down to a $0 balance before you die.

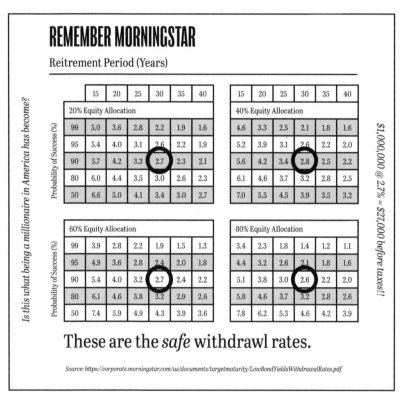

Fig. 8

Avoiding a $0 account balance before you die—that is the definition of success in this academic paper written by experts in economics and finance. Again, they don't define success as mass accumulation of funds; they define it as *the ability to maintain a balance greater than zero in your account, despite taking annual distributions at various rates at advancing ages.*

There's even more that we can take away from this Morningstar report: the impact our various investments has on our safe withdrawal rates. Looking at the chart, you'll see that there are a few different situations taken into consideration. In one column, it says *20 percent equity allocation*. The next quadrant over, it says *40 percent equity allocation*. Below that it says *60 percent*, and then *80 percent* in the far-right lower quadrant. What this is telling you is that the most you can take out of an account that's 20 percent invested in the stock market is 2.7 percent. That limit will give you 90 percent certainty that you aren't going to run out of money.

If you have 40 percent of your money invested in stocks or stock funds, Morningstar discovered that you could confidently take out 2.8 percent per year. So accumulation is good, right? The more risk you take, the more you accumulate and the higher your income could potentially be!

Except that's not the case when your objective is to receive retirement income. Look at the quadrant for those with 60 percent of their assets in the market. Their distribution rate has fallen back down to 2.7 percent. Those with 80 percent of their assets in the market are kicked back down to 2.6 percent withdrawals—and on top of that, this added risk increases your chances of losing your basis, or your principal investment, in a volatile stock market. Exceed these numbers and you are increasing your mathematical risk of going broke in retirement.

A QUICK WORD ABOUT BONDS

Bond prices are inverse to interest rates. Like kids on a playground teeter-totter, if interest rates rise, bond prices will fall.

When you think about it, a 3.67 percent required minimum distribution rate for a healthy, vigorous seventy-two-year-old doesn't sound like much. But imagine the stock and bond market as one huge portfolio. Now think about the fact that roughly ten thousand baby boomers turn 70.5 years old each day and as of January 1, 2020, under the new law, none of them will take an RMD until they reach age seventy-two. That's not going to occur until 2022—when all those baby boomers will suddenly have to start liquidating some of their holdings. Now you can see how this creates a tremendous amount of cash-flow pressure. That pressure is building—and it's only going to get worse with our aging population. Let me show you why.

REQUIRED MINIMUM DISTRIBUTION

Age	Distribution Period	Age	Distribution Period	Age	Distribution Period	Age	Distribution Period	Age	Distribution Period
70	29.1	82	18.4	94	9.5	106	4.3	118	2.5
71	28.2	83	17.6	95	8.9	107	4.1	119	2.3
72	27.3	84	16.8	96	8.3	108	3.9	120 +	2
73	26.4	85	16	97	7.8	109	3.7		
74	25.5	86	15.2	98	7.3	110	3.5		
75	24.6	87	14.4	99	6.8	111	3.4		
76	23.7	88	13.6	100	6.4	112	3.2		
77	22.8	89	12.9	101	5.9	113	3.1		
78	21.9	90	12.1	102	5.6	114	3		
79	21	91	11.4	103	5.2	115	2.9		
80	20.2	92	10.8	104	4.9	116	2.8		
81	19.3	93	10.1	105	4.6	117	2.7		

Once you determine a separate required minimum distribution from each of your traditional IRAs, you can total these minimum amounts and take them from any one or more of your traditional IRAs.

Fig. 9

By the time a baby boomer reaches age eighty, the divisor for the minimum distribution will go down (from 27.3 at seventy-two, to 20.2 at age eighty). This means that the required amount of distributions from your IRA and 401(k) account goes up. Let's see what that does to our required minimum distribution.

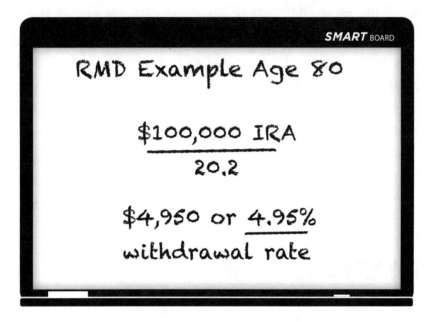

Fig. 10

If we take that same $100,000 and consider that our client is now eighty years old and we do that division, then that means the required minimum distribution now is $4,950 or 4.95 percent as a distribution rate—almost twice as much as Morningstar suggests is advisable to avoid hitting a $0 balance over a thirty-year period. And although this distribution percentage at age 80 likely sustains them for their lifetime, that's only if they are comfortable having a better-than-$1 balance remaining.

I believe that's an unsustainable amount of pressure on the market as a whole, especially in 2022. Because in that year, hundreds of thousands of new retirees whose RMDs fall under the new law will be turning seventy-two years old. And after that onslaught, we still have ten thousand more turning seventy-two every day and another ten thousand or so turning eighty years old every day. Still, you might think that's going to slow down eventually—it's not going to be ten thousand boomers turning sixty-five years old every day forever. While that's true, with advancements in medical technology, more and more retirees are living healthy and productive lives into their eighties and nineties, which means we're going to carry the burden of the boomers' forced market withdrawals for a very long time. And if the Senate successfully pushes the new plan to move the RMD to age seventy-five while forcing nonspousal beneficiaries to take the balance within five years of the IRA holder's death, imagine how high the tax rates will be on these large, inherited IRA distributions. Much higher than the parents' tax rates would have been, that much we can be confident of.

But the great salvation, say Wall Street and the economists they pay to agree, is that the millennials are coming to the party. But guess what they're strapped with? Student loan debts totaling more than $1 trillion![9] They're not even funding their own retirement plans, such as their companies' 401(k)s that invest in the stock and bond markets, because they have these large debts they've accumulated getting their education.

And it's not just the debt—it's also that millennials actively distrust the stock market. A 2015 poll conducted by Bloomberg found that almost 40 percent of millennial respondents did not trust the stock market, often citing that it is too volatile or that it wasn't fair for small investors.[10] The Great Recession of 2008 permanently scarred their young minds, as they heard countless financial horror stories from parents and relatives who lost a considerable amount of

---

9   Libby Kane, "Student Loan Debt in the US Has Topped $1.3 Trillion," Business Insider, January 12, 2016, www.businessinsider.com/student-loan-debt-state-of-the-union-2016-1.

10   Callie Bost, "Millennials Don't Trust Stock Market, Goldman Sachs Poll Shows," Bloomberg, June 24, 2015, www.bloomberg.com/news/articles/2015-06-24/millennials-don-t-trust-the-stock-market-says-goldman-sachs-poll.

retirement money to a crashing stock market. It was essentially the millennials' equivalent to the Great Depression.

All of this, in turn, leads us to this: the complete failure of traditional financial planning models at every age and in most ways.

Conversely, there's an equally detrimental trend we see with older seniors having excessive tax-deferred assets. This excess capital goes well beyond what's needed to meet their income objectives. Later, I'll share the WHERE AM I AT™ planning process. Through this process, you first identify **I**ncome needs, then for the remaining **A**ssets, you work to lower the effective **T**ax cost. Using this approach, in a well-constructed portfolio with 40 percent in equity and a fifteen-year life expectancy, 5.6 percent is safe in 90 percent of scenarios. So, for a retiree, money beyond meeting the income need should be considered for Roth conversions and/or used in a properly structured 10-pay, both of which would have a tax cost initially but accumulate tax-free afterward, without further required minimum distributions.

CHAPTER 2

THE TRUTH ABOUT THE "FUZZY" FINANCIAL MATH BANKS AND WALL STREET USE

Resulting in Traditional Financial Planning's Epic Failure to Protect Us From This Financially Flawed Math

I t's hard to swallow the truth about traditional planning's failure and what you'll soon understand as the "fuzzy" math we get from banks and Wall Street brokerage firms, but I believe you can handle it. More than that, you must be aware of the truth and dig into the realities of finance so that you don't become a victim of meaningless mathematical formulas put forth by the banks and investment brokerage community.

REVEALING THE TRUE COST (AND CONSEQUENCE) OF DEBT

Earlier, I mentioned student loan debt. Let's look deeper into that. Right now, the average borrower in the college graduating class of 2014 carries more than $33,000 in student loan debt.[11] Some may not realize how toxic this debt is to their future wealth accumulation and retirement, especially since much of it was issued with such low interest rates—but are low interest rates really that low? The answer is NO! In truth, interest rates are a big part of the tricky mathematical formulas put out by banks and financiers—a simple trick that creates incredible wealth for the banks and their largest shareholders. Let's dig in so you can see for yourself:

Amount	$100,000
Term	30 yr. 0 mo.
Rate	4.0%

What's the interest cost? 4 percent?

Are you *sure* the 4 percent rate is the cost?

Fig. 11

Imagine that you're very proud of your young grandson who is going to buy his first house for $100,000 with a thirty-year mortgage at a 4 percent interest rate. He scored this low rate because he's a hardworking young man with good credit. While you're telling your friends about his financial success, you mention his interest rate: 4

---

11   "Students & Debt," debt.org/students.

percent. You know that's his mortgage interest rate because it says so on all his loan documents, right? But as you look closer, you see that something doesn't quite add up.

Amount	**$100,000**
Term	**30 yr. 0 mo.**
Rate	**4.0%**
Monthly Payment	
	$477.22
Average Monthly Interest	
	$199.64
Total Interest	
	$71,869.51
Total Amount	
	$171,869.51

SOMETHING DOESN'T ADD UP!

Total interest: $71,869.51
Total payment: $171,869.51

41.81 percent actual interest paid
41.81 cents on every $1 paid *is interest.*

Fig. 12

If we look at the total interest your grandson is going to pay on this loan and we divide that by the total payments he makes, it's going to tell a different story. You see the word *rate* is really a mathematical function of speed. It's like when you go to your doctor and one of the nurses there, Janet, gives you a shot and, zoom, she really shoots that volume of medicine into you very quickly. In this instance, her rate is high, or very fast. It's a quotient of speed. But then you have another nurse, Mary, who puts that shot into your arm and very slowly injects the medication. It's the same amount of medication, but it takes a lot longer this time around. That is what rate is all about—the speed.

Yet, what really matters isn't the speed or velocity but the *volume* of medicine you get. The right amount will help you get better, but too much and you're dead. Volume is also what matters when you look at the interest you actually pay. It's really the total amount of interest out of your pocket—not the annual percentage rate—that tells the true story of what the loan costs.

When we look at volume of interest, we need to look at something a little different than just the rate. We need to look at the total amount of interest paid. In the case of your hypothetical grandson, a $100,000 mortgage over thirty years at a 4 percent interest rate equals $71,869.51 in interest over the full term of the loan. Add that interest amount to the $100,000 that your grandson borrowed and the total amount of payments is $171,869.51.

So what is the actual percentage of interest paid on every dollar? A horrifying 41.81 percent. That's how I look at it. If I'm paying a dollar, how much is going to interest? Well, it actually costs the borrower 41.81 cents of every dollar paid to satisfy the interest payments. And this really is a best-case scenario, because most people don't keep a thirty-year mortgage for thirty years. If you're familiar with how amortization works, you'll know that there's more interest paid in the early years. So if you refinance every seven to nine years, these interest rates could easily exceed 60 percent.

Another detrimental choice being foisted on today's society is leasing. Leasing is a way for dealers to get younger folks to basically agree to a lifetime payment in exchange for never owning a thing. It's 100 percent interest not amortized because all of it goes for use and none of it for ownership.

When you get down to it, few people really understand amortization. It's not uncommon for someone with a 3.5 percent interest rate to believe they are financially ahead if their 401(k) is up 7 percent. But they are not! Far from it.

Let's consider a $30,000, ten-year term student loan at 4.79 percent. What is the interest cost on that first payment? Here's the math:

$$(30,000 \times .0479) / 12$$

$$1437/12$$

$$\$119.75 \text{ interest}$$

With a payment of $315.13, the first payment puts $119.75 toward interest, which is an effective interest cost of 38 percent.

Bankers use this math trick to ensure that consumers don't fully see the impact of debt. This process also makes it almost impossible for consumers to get free from the cycle of debt without extreme cost. In turn, this reduces their savings power and their overall wealth potential, which I refer to as Lifetime Economic Earnings Velocity, making retirement planning that much more difficult.

We all know that the earlier we start saving, the more money we will eventually have. Look at this chart:

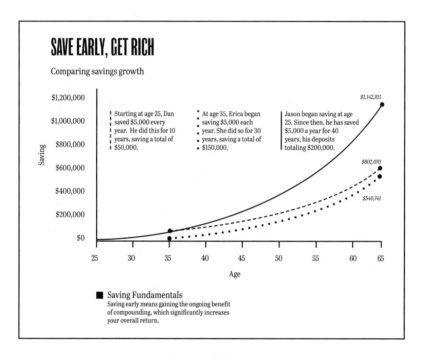

Fig. 13

In reviewing this chart, you realize that the mantra we should all live by is: **Start Early, Get Rich!** But the banks make that hard to do when people face actual interest costs between 20 and 60 percent on mortgages, auto loans, student loans, credit cards, and business debts. If you're a business-owning parent or grandparent, the best thing you can do is hire your kids and grandkids and encourage them to put a portion of their earnings into a

Roth IRA. Since they won't earn enough to pay income taxes, these tax-free contributions end up being tax-free distributions decades later. Do this little thing, and you'll have tax-free millionaires in your family a few decades from now.

Losing lifetime economic earnings velocity is a huge problem that's not just restricted to young people. Retirees and preretirees are also victims, with many of them in a race to pay off their house or car, only to find themselves dragging the even more harmful credit card debt into retirement.

The solution is a SMART approach to debt elimination using a strategy we call *Debt Free 4 Life*™. In this strategy, you invest into tax-exempt assets the amount you'd normally pay over the minimum payments due on your debt. These funds then continue to compound as you "snowball" your debt away. The SMART Debt Free 4 Life™ process tackles the lowest-balance debts first using funds that have flowed through a high-cash-value life insurance policy. This means the contribution amount, which is equal to a normal debt repayment, grows, much like a snowball rolling downhill. It knocks out a growing amount of debt without requiring any more of your money than you were paying out before to the banks, credit card issuers, auto lenders, and student loan lenders.

Meanwhile, in your accumulated savings created with this specially designed insurance contract, your funds continue to compound after all the debts are paid. Because the debts are paid much faster than the bank's payment schedule, you save a fortune in interest payments while gaining accumulated savings within the cash-value policy.

This SMART method allows dollars to continue to compound so when you need to make future purchases, you can do so with your own cash instead of costly credit. In essence, going through this cycle of debt and adding accumulated savings will allow you to live debt-free off your own cash. When you do, you'll become Debt Free 4 Life™.

If you treat the accumulated savings like you would a bank and make comparable payments when you use the accumulated capital, your wealth will continuously compound for the remainder of your life. So many retirees and pre-retirees don't realize that finding the right approach to debt elimination and major postretirement purchases is likely more important than funding their 401(k) beyond the match. They mismanage their cash flow and debts—often trying to target a pay-off date without factoring in or even understanding how the volume of compounding interest works against them.

The trick is to understand the truth about amortized debt and snowball it away—something your local bank, which benefits from all the interest you pay, certainly won't share with you.

Recently we developed a Debt Free 4 Life™ plan for a client who was paying on a fifteen-year mortgage with twelve years remaining until the mortgage would be paid off. They had a home equity line of credit and over

$20,000 of credit card debt with only five years left before his desired retirement age.

By using the Debt Free 4 Life™ approach, he will be debt-free with $54,000 of extra cash left in his "bank" of accumulated cash value before his ideal retirement date. In addition, his family will have paid-up life insurance that his wife, a few years younger, knows she can count on.

Also important to note is that traditional debt snowballing would have paid their debts eight months faster than Debt Free 4 Life™, but if they wanted a new car, they would have to again borrow from the bank. With DF4L, they now have flipped the compounding interest in their favor.

She can then live off tax-free assets and support her income needs throughout her remaining retirement years, without required minimum distributions, allowing his retirement assets to better serve her and continue to compound tax-free for their children when she passes. This all happens at the lowest possible effective tax cost and lowest possible interest cost based on their financial situation.

Your SMART Advisor Network Member has given you access to the SMART debt elimination plan calculator at:

www.DebtFree4Life.com

Refer to the first page of this book for your access code to see these reader-only, passcode protected resources.

Use this resource and guidance so you'll be the only financier you ever need for future major financial purchases or "loans." Use Debt Free 4 Life™ and you'll be the only honest source of money you'll ever need and your money will continuously compound for you!

The advisor who gave you this book has access to our exclusive Debt Free 4 Life Debt Elimination Plan report generating system. Ask them to provide you with a personalized plan showing a breakdown of the true, effective interest cost of your debt and your estimated Debt Free 4 Life™ timeline and savings. Not only will this illustrate how much you can save on lifetime interest expenses but it also estimates the accumulated cash values you could gain toward future financial needs/purchases.

To see a sample Debt Free 4 Life Debt Elimination Plan report, visit the Appendix.

THE RATE OF RETURN MYTH

We spend our early lives working to set aside more assets—to essentially climb the mountain of asset accumulation—so that when we retire, we have the funds to help us get back down the mountain. But as you just learned, Wall Street's fuzzy math and the convenient misrepresentation of the true nature of interest on debt encourages us to ignore debt as what it truly is: a huge obstacle to accumulation. A boulder in the path up that mountain.

But that's not all you have to contend with! At the same time as the truth about debt is being misrepresented, we can easily fall victim to yet another mathematical trick carried out by the folks on Wall Street, and it's called rate of return. Their trick has been convincing us that all that really matters is how much rate of return we're earning.

Now, rate of return has some validity to it, but it's only half the story. If I said to you, "Hey, look, there's a giant mountain with snow-capped peaks rising up for miles—as far as the eye can see. Let's go climb it," what would our true objective be? Just to get to the top of the mountain, or would it be to get to the top of the mountain, take our pictures, celebrate our success, and then scale back down safely so we can go home? Naturally, no one wants to plan only to climb the mountain—they want to also plan to get back down safely.

Retirement planning is a lot like climbing a mountain. In preretirement, during your accumulation stage, rate of return is significant. It represents your climb up the mountain. But in the distribution phase—that time when you're actually shifting into retirement and you're starting to get income from your assets—the math changes dramatically.

What if a financial advisor told you they had this amazing crystal ball that was never wrong and they proved it to you? They say, "Your Aunt May is going to call you right now," and the phone rings and sure enough, it is Aunt May. Then they say your cousin will win the lottery tomorrow, and she does. Then you and the advisor do a few more things like this until you have complete faith in the crystal ball. If after proving all that to you, the advisor tells you that they were looking into the crystal ball and saw that the stock market was going to earn an average of 14.84 percent over the next thirty years, you'd be excited, right? Why wouldn't you be? I'd be excited, too.

Let's check this retirement out and talk about how well that crystal ball did for you.

THE DANGERS OF AN AVERAGE RATE OF RETURN

Beginning retirement asset value	=	$1,000,000	10% of beginning value	=	($100,000)
Number of years	=	30	Average return	=	14.84%

Constant Returns

Retirement Year	Annual Return	Annual Income	Account Value
1	14.84%	-$100,000	$1,033,290
2	14.84%	-$100,000	$1,072,100
3	14.84%	-$100,000	$1,116,360
4	14.84%	-$100,000	$1,167,188
5	14.84%	-$100,000	$1,225,558
6	14.84%	-$100,000	$1,292,591
7	14.84%	-$100,000	$1,369,572
8	14.84%	-$100,000	$1,457,976
9	14.84%	-$100,000	$1,559,500
10	14.84%	-$100,000	$1,676,090
11	14.84%	-$100,000	$1,809,982
12	14.84%	-$100,000	$1,963,743
13	14.84%	-$100,000	$2,140,322
14	14.84%	-$100,000	$2,343,106
15	14.84%	-$100,000	$2,575,983
20	14.84%	-$100,000	$4,373,434
25	14.84%	-$100,000	$7,963,668
30	14.84%	-$100,000	$15,134,818

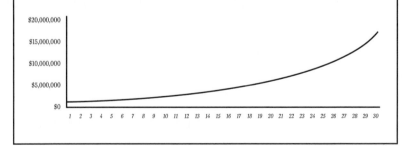

Fig. 14

Thanks to the crystal ball, you're going to take $1 million and assume a constant rate of return of 14.84 percent and, being the smart conservative adult you are, you decide to just take $100,000 out every year. After ten years, you will have taken out $1 million of income and you'd still have $1.676 million in your account. Not only did you get to enjoy $1 million of income and the retirement lifestyle it buys, but you also grew your wealth by more than $676,000. After twenty years, it gets even better. You've taken out $2 million, but that little bit extra that you've left behind has compounded, all the way to $4.3 million. What a plan, right? After thirty years, your family's around you in your giant mansion, you've taken $3 million of income out, and you're leaving a massive amount of wealth—to the tune of $15.134 million—to your loved ones. Three million dollars in income and $15 million to the family—all because the crystal ball was never wrong.

But maybe we're jumping to conclusions here without analyzing all the facts. Because the crystal ball never told us how that 14.84 percent was actually earned. It just said over the next thirty years, the market would average 14.84 percent. Now, if we were in the accumulation phase for thirty years, that would be great. But if we're in the distribution phase—climbing down that mountain after saving for retirement—then the actual numbers look quite different.

Let's take a look at the real numbers and see what happens if we actually tried to implement the "crystal ball" plan.

CONSTANT VS. FLUCTUATING RETURNS

Range of years   =   1970-1999   *Average* return   =   14.84%

History of the S&P 500

Year	Annual Return	Year	Annual Return
1970	3.99%	1985	31.65%
1971	14.33%	1986	18.60%
1972	18.94%	1987	5.17%
1973	-14.79%	1988	16.61%
1974	-26.54%	1989	31.69%
1975	37.25%	1990	-3.10%
1976	23.67%	1991	30.47%
1977	-7.39%	1992	7.62%
1978	6.44%	1993	10.08%
1979	18.35%	1994	1.32%
1980	32.27%	1995	37.58%
1981	-5.05%	1996	22.96%
1982	21.48%	1997	33.36%
1983	22.50%	1998	28.58%
1984	6.15%	1999	21.04%

Fig. 15

First off, you notice that the word *average* is italicized above? That's because the stock market doesn't offer us a static, fixed return—it offers us a fluctuating return. The crystal ball was definitely correct, but once you begin taking income, rate of return is no longer the focal point. Something new matters, and that's called *sequence of returns.*

When you have variable investments in your retirement accounts, such as bonds, mutual funds, ETFs, and stocks, their returns fluctuate based on a variety of reasons far outside your control, such as perceived value, demand, news events, earnings reports, interest rates, politics, and more. If you have low or negative returns in the early years and you maintain normal distributions, then you deplete your capital before it has a chance to replenish itself. By the time the higher returns happen, you have already drained the account by so much that there is not enough left in your account to grow sufficiently to help you maintain that lifetime income or to protect your principal balance—which means you lose both.

This, essentially, is the problem with sequence of return risk.

THE REAL RISK: SEQUENCE OF RETURNS

Beginning retirement asset value = $1,000,000   10% of beginning value = ($100,000)
Number of years = 30   Average return = 14.84%

Fluctuating Returns

Year	Annual Return	Annual Income	Account Value
1	3.99%	-$100,000	$935,910
2	14.33%	-$100,000	$955,696
3	18.94%	-$100,000	$1,017,765
4	-14.79%	-$100,000	$782,027
5	-26.54%	-$100,000	$501,017
6	37.25%	-$100,000	$550,396
7	23.67%	-$100,000	$557,005
8	-7.39%	-$100,000	$423,232
9	6.44%	-$100,000	$344,048
10	18.35%	-$100,000	$288,831
11	32.27%	-$100,000	$249,767
12	-5.05%	-$100,000	$142,204
13	21.48%	-$100,000	$51,269
14	22.50%	-$51,269	$0
15	6.15%	$0	$0

Fig. 16

Let's try to implement our plan now with a fluctuating rate of return. In year 1, you're down quite a bit. So you call the advisor and say, "I've got my $100,000 income this year, but I'm down to $935,000 here. I'm a little nervous." The advisor tells you not to worry, it will come back, it's just that kind of year and besides, the advisor says, the market always comes back. And because you saw that crystal ball, which you know to be accurate, you believe the advisor.

The next year you take another $100,000 out, so you have now had $200,000 of retirement income taken from this account, and your balance does go up to $955,000. You think, "This is headed in the right direction. It's actually working out."

In year 3, you take another $100,000 and your balance shoots up to over $1 million. Now you're at the country club and you're with your friends and you're telling them how amazing your financial advisor is with their crystal ball. You brag to your golfing buddies that you've taken out $300,000 over the past three years, yet you're actually at a gain on your $1 million investment. They look at you in awe, thinking they must go see your advisor, right?

Well, year 4 comes around. It's 1973 and, bam, you're down 14 percent. You take $100,000 out, as usual, and at the end of the year, your balance is $782,027. You call your advisor and say, "Whoa, I'm really nervous here." Your advisor says, "Remember what happened last time? This is just a bigger correction. You need to hold on and it's going to come back."

But that's not what happens. Instead, the next year rolls around and you take out your next $100,000 and the market tanks another 26 percent—and your balance is down to $500,000 and, from your perspective, you've lost half of your money. For the vast majority of us, that's the "uncle" point. We're done and we cry, "Uncle!" We are going to take that money out, put it in a CD, and live a very meager existence in retirement because of the tremendous amount of wealth that we've just lost.

But if you're stubborn—I had one uncle who was stubborn as a mule. He'd have probably said, "I'm just going to keep getting my $100,000 out. It's supposed to work, the crystal ball said so," and he would keep taking it. If you were stubborn like him, you would see that by year 13, you have lost all your money.

This really illustrates the significant difference that rate of return plays when considering accumulation compared to distribution. If the sequence of returns is poor and you are fully invested in variable return assets, then you have the very real possibility of losing all of your money.

When you need that retirement income, or are required to take income (RMDs) from your retirement accounts, if you want to keep your money intact, then you have to be smarter about how you approach your distributions in the future.

 In a 2016 Forbes article, Wade Pfau, professor of retirement income at the American College, wrote, "Taking distributions from an investment portfolio amplifies the impact of portfolio volatility, making retirement income planning particularly tricky, as distributions tend to be the primary income source for retirees."[12] In the good years,

---

12   Wade Pfau, "Weighing Sequence of Returns Risk for Retirees," *Forbes*, August 2, 2016, www.forbes.com/sites/wadepfau/2016/08/02/weighing-sequence-of-returns-risk-for-retirees/#6875d830f242.

when the market never seems to stop climbing, the idea of performance being amplified sounds pretty good.

But in the bad years, like in 2008, when the bottom just seemed to fall out of the financial world, amplified volatility can spell disaster for retirees who have no time—or income— to reinvest and recover from losses.

In 2016, when talking about sequence of returns risk in another article, Pfau wrote, "The financial market returns experienced near retirement matter a great deal more than most people realize. Even with the same average returns over a long period of time, retiring at the start of a bear market is very dangerous; wealth can be rapidly depleted as withdrawals are made from a diminishing portfolio, leaving little money to benefit from a subsequent market recovery."[13]

Yet, how can a retiree plan to retire and begin taking distributions at the right time? A time when the market is rising—not losing? Frankly, they can't. But what they **can** do is build in a volatility buffer. Ask any smart actuary, a professional who knows numbers at the highest level, what a pensioner should have, and they'll say an annuity. Annuities, in appropriate amounts, are the very best volatility buffer you can own. Think of the 60/40 approach in terms of stocks and annuities, not bonds.

---

13   Wade Pfau, "Navigating One of the Greatest Risks of Retirement Income Planning," *Forbes*, June 20, 2016, www.forbes.com/sites/wadepfau/2016/06/20/navigating-one-of-the-greatest-risks-of-retirement-income-planning/#5b7fac575fc1.

We have to remember, too, that Morningstar is telling us it doesn't really matter if we're 20 percent, 40 percent, 60 percent, or even 80 percent in the stock market, the amount we can withdraw is relatively similar, falling somewhere between 2.6 and 2.8 percent over a thirty-year postretirement life expectancy. When we were new in the business, the industry powers that be taught advisors that everything was about our asset allocation. Heck, the creators of the concept of asset allocation won a Nobel Prize in 1990.[14] But we've since learned from experience that this isn't completely true.

Taking 2.7 percent on $1 million is $27,000. Is this what being a millionaire in America has become? And if it's in a traditional IRA or 401(k) account, then that's before taxes. How are we going to make ends meet if we believe taxes are going up? How do we make ends meet if we believe that health insurance is going to become exponentially more expensive in the future? How are we going to make our money last?

Your SMART Advisor Network Member has given you access to a game with a fun way to show you how fluctuating returns and sequence of returns risk will impact your retirement savings.

To get started visit: www.SecureIncome4Life.com

Refer to the first page of this book for your access code to see these reader-only, passcode-protected resources.

---

14   "This Year's Laureates Are Pioneers in the Theory of Financial Economics and Corporate Finance," October 16, 1990, www.nobelprize.org/nobel_prizes/economic-sciences/laureates/1990/press.html.

Secure Income 4 Life™ is a retirement "game" of chance. The returns shown are based on the actual price change of the S&P 500 in any chosen year, a participation rate in a hypothetical balanced index reflective of options available in the market based again on a specific year, and a fixed rate of return selected by you.

The game is easy—just choose a card and you'll see that year's performance.

As you play, the average rate of return will adjust, as will your account balance. Your balance will move based on the income needs you've set as you progress toward and through retirement over the next twenty years.

The best part is the results are completely random! Crazy math fact: Your balance has 2,432,902,008,176,640,000 different potential outcomes! That's 2.432 quintillion possibilities. What will shock you is, at some point, your balance will be higher with a lower average rate of return. Play this game—it will help you understand the most important aspect of retirement income planning.

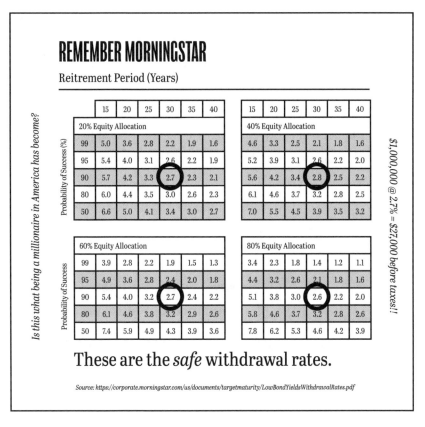

Is this what being a millionaire in America has become?

REMEMBER MORNINGSTAR

Reitrement Period (Years)

Probability of Success (%)

	15	20	25	30	35	40
20% Equity Allocation						
99	5.0	3.6	2.8	2.2	1.9	1.6
95	5.4	4.0	3.1	2.6	2.2	1.9
90	5.7	4.2	3.3	2.7	2.3	2.1
80	6.0	4.4	3.5	3.0	2.6	2.3
50	6.6	5.0	4.1	3.4	3.0	2.7

	15	20	25	30	35	40
40% Equity Allocation						
99	4.6	3.3	2.5	2.1	1.8	1.6
95	5.2	3.9	3.1	2.6	2.2	2.0
90	5.6	4.2	3.4	2.8	2.5	2.2
80	6.1	4.6	3.7	3.2	2.8	2.5
50	7.0	5.5	4.5	3.9	3.5	3.2

Probability of Success

	15	20	25	30	35	40
60% Equity Allocation						
99	3.9	2.8	2.2	1.9	1.5	1.3
95	4.9	3.6	2.8	2.4	2.0	1.8
90	5.4	4.0	3.2	2.7	2.4	2.2
80	6.1	4.6	3.8	3.2	2.9	2.6
50	7.4	5.9	4.9	4.3	3.9	3.6

	15	20	25	30	35	40
80% Equity Allocation						
99	3.4	2.3	1.8	1.4	1.2	1.1
95	4.4	3.2	2.6	2.1	1.8	1.6
90	5.1	3.8	3.0	2.6	2.2	2.0
80	5.8	4.6	3.7	3.2	2.8	2.6
50	7.8	6.2	5.3	4.6	4.2	3.9

$1,000,000 @ 2.7% = $27,000 before taxes!!

These are the *safe* withdrawal rates.

Source: https://corporate.morningstar.com/us/documents/targetmaturity/LowBondYieldsWithdrawalRates.pdf

Fig. 17

Obviously, we can't make these low retirement income distribution rates work, and on top of it, we have to be smart about how big a role we allow taxes to play in our net income—because in that, we are not powerless. Our future taxes, and the amount we lose to poor cash-flow management, are a direct result of the choices we make now.

The WHERE AM I AT™ planning process mentioned earlier and further explained in a later chapter is an approach that can help you tax diversify and increase the after-tax value of a portion of your assets. We can change some of our assets to a tax-free status now and make the asset more valuable over time as it compounds. You see, all the financial decisions you make now have a compounding effect on your future liabilities and the net after-tax value of your assets.

That's why we need to work on the Strategic Movement Around Retirement Taxation®—in order to have a positive compounding effect by better managing our future tax liabilities now—today! Because the tax code's pretty clear: you have a legal obligation to pay tax once. Yet many of the decisions made by people today (based on the advice of their tax-UNaware advisors) make them pay taxes over and over and over again, robbing them of valuable compounding on those dollars they've lost to taxes on their journey to retirement.

Now For The Rest Of The Sequence Of Return Story

In my opinion, advisors today have made it a habit to explain the ill-effects of a negative sequence of return on future retirement income, and they definitely should. But what happens when you start out with a FANTASTIC year? Imagine for a moment, you work with your SMART advisor and they calculate the amount of your IRA that you can convert to Roth; the conversion carries a 20.37 percent tax cost. You might think that converting is a mistake because of the tax cost, but let's take a look at the actual numbers when you have a great return on your investment that year.

$100,000 IRA conversion tax cost = $20,370.

Net Roth IRA balance (assuming taxes withheld from the IRA assets) = $79,630.

In the next 12 months your return is abnormal but abnormally good = 25%

Year end Roth Balance is $99,537.50, a net difference of $462.50.

Which is more valuable: a $100,000 IRA or a $99,537.50 Roth IRA?

The Roth has no additional tax due and even if the $100,000 IRA belongs to someone with no other income and they cash out, the income tax will be greater than $462.50.

Roth wins!

Another giant consideration regarding sequence of returns is the amount of time left in retirement. Consider this: Is a seventy-two-year-old with a $3,000,000 IRA and modest supplemental retirement income needs with a healthy defined benefit pension a good candidate to do an IRA to Roth IRA conversion? Perhaps, yes, because the income need dictates how the remaining assets should be managed from a tax-aware perspective.

This seventy-two-year-old has SMART options. Why not convert the excess capital to a tax-free asset like a Roth? Or how about an insurance-based product with a tax-free death benefit beyond the effective tax cost? Moves like these can add millions to the value left for a spouse and family, and they have no negative effect on the retiree's retirement income and lifestyle.

ROTH Conversion Later™

Not everyone wants to do a Roth conversion now and pay taxes out of their savings today. For those who want to reduce the cost of a future Roth conversion, we have the Roth Conversion Later™ plan. Ask the advisor who gave you this book for your free, personalized report showing how we can lower the total effective tax cost of your future Roth conversion and create an added, tax-free death benefit for your loved ones.

To see a sample Roth Conversion Later™ plan report, visit the Appendix.

When you consider the difference in returns between a fixed-rate product and one that fluctuates, you might start wondering where you can get a fixed-rate product with that impressive a return. The truth is, you can't. The good news, however, is you really don't need to.

Think about it this way: a return could be substantially lower than the 14.84 percent used in the example and it would still help you maintain an ongoing balance of about $1 million while taking income distributions as high as $54,000 per year (depending on your age and prevailing interest rates). Is it worth it to risk it all to try to grow your account to an unrealistic $15 million in thirty years when your goal, really, is to receive a comfortable, continual, tax-advantaged, completely spendable income stream while maintaining your principal, which is what most people want out of their personal retirement plan?

Fixed products, such as bonds (which are fixed on income but not value), fixed insurance-based products, and money market accounts typically have lower returns than other stock market-based investments. That's because they are lower in risk. Some are even guaranteed— something no stock market-based investment offers.

But that lowered risk helps to better ensure that you can get the return of your capital. And there's even more good news! When you're retired, you're living off the withdrawal rate, not the rate of return you've gotten while accumulating your money. So it's more important to find ways to guarantee the safety of a portion of your capital and ensure its return than it is to find a high yield (with corresponding high risk).

Why? In part because a higher yield means more fluctuation and, as we discussed, that volatility can completely wipe you out. There are ways to plan around a lower, more conservative return in your early retirement years so that your withdrawals are more efficient on an after-effective-tax cost basis through tax-aware planning techniques, which we'll discuss in more detail in the next chapter.

Remember, an asset's true value is its worth AFTER the tax is paid. A $1,000,000 IRA is NOT worth as much as a $1,000,000 Roth IRA. Not even close.

Did you know that a dollar you get today is worth more than a dollar you get tomorrow? It's true. A concept called *the time value of money* teaches us that a dollar you receive today has time to earn interest and compound and has more spending power than it will in a year when inflation has increased the costs of goods and services. This concept helps us understand why it's so important that you manage your inevitable future tax liabilities and that you truly understand what you're getting—or not getting—in terms of net real return AFTER tax.

To illustrate how average rates of return can be confusing, I want to do some Wall Street mathematical wizardry. To do this, let's look at some simple math.

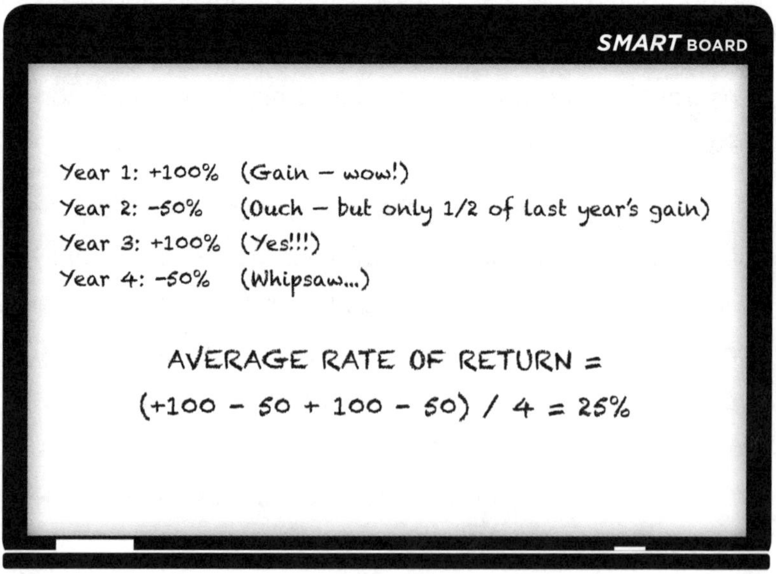

SMART BOARD

Year 1: +100% (Gain — wow!)
Year 2: -50% (Ouch — but only 1/2 of last year's gain)
Year 3: +100% (Yes!!!)
Year 4: -50% (Whipsaw....)

AVERAGE RATE OF RETURN =
(+100 - 50 + 100 - 50) / 4 = 25%

Fig. 18

An average return of 25 percent is nothing to complain about, and it certainly should improve the value of your money in the future. Now let's see how this looks when we turn this hefty average return into real money with, say, $10,000 invested.

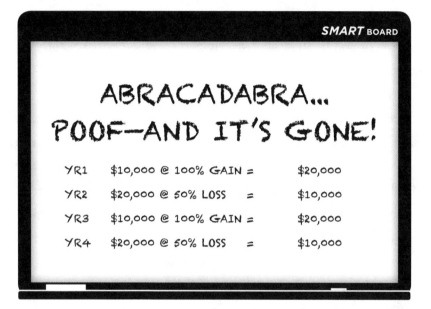

Fig. 19

While it's true that the average rate of return was 25 percent, it's also true that you got zero growth on your $10,000 investment. Beware of Wall Street math wizardry! To see this concept at work in your own portfolio, remember to play the game at SecureIncome4Life.com.

PLANNING YOUR DESCENT: MORE IMPORTANT THAN THE CLIMB

I can't imagine anyone looking forward to being stranded at the top of a mountain they just worked so hard to climb. I also can't imagine any retiree working hard to save and preserve money during their career just so they can pay a big chunk in taxes just a few years after retirement and be left stranded, relying heavily on Social Security to get them through.

There are many challenges facing us as we work to create a lasting, tax-efficient retirement plan, but there are ways to still accomplish this despite the obstacles. In the next chapter, I'll introduce you to SMART Planz, a unique approach to creating a more tax-aware 401(k) plan and an optimal way for self-employed entrepreneurs to strategically move around retirement taxation. SMART Planz gives the self-employed the ability to save smarter for their retirement so they can enjoy greater, ongoing financial independence and gain comfortable peace of mind.

A tax-aware approach works for everyone. If you're still working, you can improve your future tax efficiency by being SMART today. Already retired? You too can get SMART with your money and enhance the income you receive or the estate you leave.

It's time to learn a SMARTer way.

CHAPTER 3

USING BASIS AND FLOAT TO GAIN FINANCIAL FREEDOM

et's talk about what it means to have a SMART Retirement. To us, SMART means ensuring that your money makes a Strategic Movement Around Retirement Taxation®. The goal here is to help maximize your after-tax retirement income over what conventional traditional financial planning can provide, while targeting as low a tax rate as possible in your retirement and eliminating any debts you have as quickly as possible. It makes sense that we should target as low a tax bracket as we possibly can so that the majority of your retirement income is spendable and received without owing any money on net-spendable, income-reducing debt.

You've no doubt noticed that today, everyone has smartphones and smart TVs. But what about smart money? What can we do to make the money that we have smarter? How can we make it work better and have more functionality in our future retirement years?

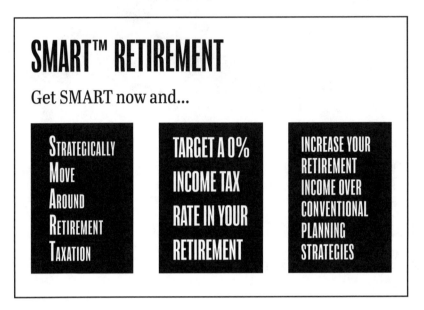

Fig. 20

IT'S SMART TO KNOW YOUR BASIS

Will Rogers is credited as having said, "I am not so much concerned with the return on my capital as I am with the return of my capital." This is a quote that really highlights what I think has been lost along the way, especially by 401(k) providers, and that is that the word *basis* means a lot. If we were a bunch of accountants reading this, we would all know exactly what basis means. Since we're not, let me explain.

Basis is the amount of capital we've actually paid in. It is the total amount we have put into each investment—it's our outlay of capital. It's funny how frequently I run into somebody who has a 401(k) plan, and when I ask them how much they've invested into their 401(k) account, they want to tell me a percentage and how much the company matches. But I say, "No, no, no. How much money have you contributed in dollars?" And almost nobody ever has an answer to that question.

To create a SMART plan, we really need to understand what our basis paid in is and how to make our money work beyond that basis.

Of course, knowing how much you've contributed doesn't, in and of itself, ensure that you will get all of it back or manage its growth well. But what it does ensure is that you can create a plan to secure all the capital you've contributed—a way to neutralize losses and make sure the full amount of your capital remains accessible to you in retirement.

A few decades ago, this wasn't as important. Back then, most employers, even those in the private sector, had pension plans set up for employees. Pension plans are also called defined benefit plans because they are established with the purpose of paying out a set monthly payment to retirees. Because retirees could count on those payments, and because they were fully funded by the employer—with absolutely no money paid in by the employees—there was no need to be concerned about the basis.

Likewise, there was no need to be concerned about future retirement income. The pension plan was funded for you, based on your salary and years of service. It was a simple plan that put all of the investment risk and responsibility on your employer.

Now things have changed. Employers have embraced a different model for retirement planning: the defined contribution plan. In this model, the employee contributes a certain amount of their pay, chosen by them, and the company may or may not match a portion of that contribution. Worse, the employees have to make all the investment decisions.

But we're not done yet. Losses in the account are losses of your money—and those losses negatively impact your potential future income. There is no guaranteed payout for the retiree to count on. That means it's absolutely crucial to understand what you've invested in and exactly how much your basis is—to define how much you've contributed—so you can make sure that amount is working for you and, as Will Rogers advises, it will eventually be returned to you in the form of retirement income, we hope, with significant gains.

Right now, I want to discuss the word *float*. If you've ever read anything about Warren Buffett, the most successful investor in our country, then you may know that profiting from insurance float is something that he has focused Berkshire Hathaway on. We too can be like Buffett and profit from understanding how actuaries price different types of insurance products so that we can get a greater return, significantly reduce risk, and achieve a lower tax liability.

Warren Buffett, founder and majority stockholder of the holding company Berkshire Hathaway, is our country's most successful and celebrated investor. As you can imagine, it takes an incredible amount of insight, courage, and knowledge to reach the heights of success that he has. One of the ways he's been so successful is by shunning conventionally accepted interpretations of investing and accounting and, instead, looking at the math of a situation and capitalizing on the story it tells. This is how Buffett was able to recognize and use the profit potential of float:

And he doesn't keep this secret to himself. He is so impressed with the way float has helped him grow his wealth, he mentions the term forty-six times in his 2015 letter to Berkshire Hathaway shareholders. Plus, that's not the first time he's mentioned it. Here's what he said about float in his 2014 shareholder letter:

So how does our float affect intrinsic value? When Berkshire's book value is calculated, the full amount of our float is deducted as a liability, just as if we had to pay it out tomorrow and could not replenish it. But to think of float as strictly a liability is incorrect; it should instead be viewed as a revolving fund.[15]

You and I may not be on Warren Buffett's level, but we can still try to understand float and use it in our own SMART plans as a revolving fund for major purchases and future income. Float is, essentially, the money an insurance company has in reserve to pay out future claims.

You see, insurance companies routinely collect premiums, yet rarely pay these premiums out in claims immediately since most claims are made far into the future. To capitalize on the time lag between the date they collect premiums and the far future date they have to pay those premiums back out as claims, insurance companies invest the premium dollars and earn interest. So, as Buffett tells us, accountants have to look at that float as a liability since it may eventually be paid out as a claim.

---

15   "2014 Annual Report," Berkshire Hathaway, Inc., www.berkshirehathaway.com/2014ar/2014ar.pdf.

But for him—and for us—it's possible to continue to collect interest on that money. Because of this, Buffett believes the market is undervaluing his huge company since current accounting rules don't recognize the true value of his company's float as an asset. This is similar to the way most people look at a life insurance or annuity premium as a bill. Done the smart way, like Buffett, this "bill" helps you build a fully accessible revolving fund!

SMART is a two-pronged approach to successful retirement planning. When people ask me what I do, I tell them I make people tax aware and educate them on ways to lower their effective tax cost in retirement. By becoming tax aware, my clients discover the differences between the current tax status of their assets, and this opens up a potential tax arbitrage opportunity.

Arbitrage is a big, fancy word but all it means is that there are profitable advantages to different types of assets. Imagine buying a used car for $500 from a seller who's desperate to get rid of it and at the same time having a signed agreement in hand to sell it to an eager buyer across town with a cashier's check for $700. That's arbitrage.

That's what we're going to focus on—how to take a profitable advantage of differences in tax rates using low- to no-risk, insurance-based products in a complementary way that's different than the way these products are traditionally marketed to the public.

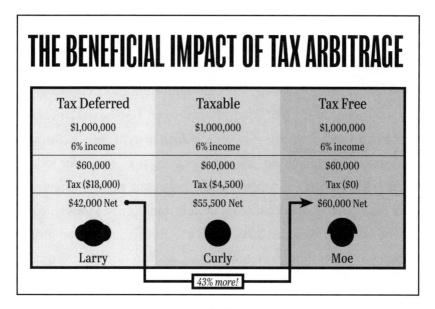

Fig. 21

Let's get into the nitty-gritty of tax awareness by using the Three Stooges as an example. Say hello to Larry, Curly, and Moe.

Larry was always the smart one. His accou ntant told him to put his money away in a tax-deferred plan, so he did. His advisor helped him grow his money well, so he wasn't too worried about his future retirement. Based on market conditions and interest rates, he grew his retirement to $1,000,000 and, at retirement, was able to take 6 percent out each year. What Larry didn't know was what his tax rate would be at that point. But he was told, as so many are, that he would be in a lower tax bracket in his retirement years, and he trusted that information.

Curly preferred to pay tax on the money he earned and buy individual company stocks, so he invested in the stock market and kept track of his cost basis. He put money into a regular taxable brokerage account and knew that when he took the money out, he would have to pay capital gains on the growth while also paying income tax on the dividends he collected along the way. Like Larry, Curly expected to take out around 6 percent because that was the prevailing interest rate at the time.

Moe, on the other hand, was always a little more conservative. He was worried he'd make a "dumb" investment, so he paid his taxes, then put his money into a safe, simple savings-type vehicle through an insurance company into a Roth IRA, which allowed him to take tax-free distributions of 6 percent (the prevailing interest rate at the time) once he retired. Even though he occasionally had a lower growth rate, he knew he wouldn't have to deal with the unpredictability of future markets or future taxes. Now let's see how this worked out:

- It looks like Larry, with his tax-deferred savings, got the most taxing result. Taking out $60,000 gross income and being forced to pay ordinary income taxes on that income leaves him with just $42,000 to spend each year.

- Curly did better with his taxable account because he'd already paid the tax on his cost basis when he first invested. Since the capital gains tax rate was lower than the income tax rate when he took distributions, this left him with $55,500 to spend each year.

- But it's Moe who really found the simplest, most effective way to plan his retirement. For him, there is no tax on the $60,000 annual withdrawal, leaving him with the full $60,000 to spend each year—43 percent more income than Larry.

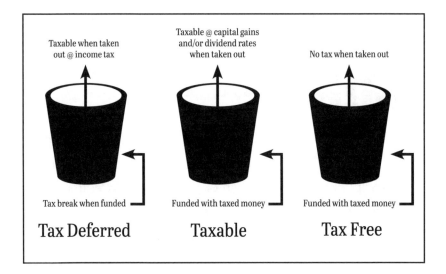

Fig. 22

Take a look at figure 22 and imagine that you could take your retirement income from any one of these three buckets. Which would you choose? Would you choose the tax-deferred bucket, which guarantees that you'll have to pay taxes on the money you take out in the future? Would you choose the taxable bucket and have to pay taxes on your gains and on dividends when they're paid (even if you don't take the cash out of your account)? Or would you choose the tax-free bucket—the only one that legally allows you to keep all the money you take out, without sharing any of your gains with the IRS?

It makes sense that it's generally best to have your money coming out of the lowest-taxed vehicle when possible so that more of your retirement income is spendable.

If you've read many books or websites that talk about financial planning, you may have heard about the bucket strategy of retirement planning. The idea generally boils down to having assets spread out over two to three "buckets," one in cash or highly liquid investments so that you can pay for short-term needs and expenses, one with longer-term investments that are still relatively low risk (or no risk) so you can use them for needs within the first five to ten years of retirement, and one with higher-potential, more volatile, tax-deferred positions for far-off, long-term income needs.

This can be a valid asset allocation strategy, but without careful planning, the second and third buckets could be highly exposed to taxation once the assets are distributed. Ultimately, it doesn't matter how many buckets you split your assets into if each of the buckets has an ever-growing, IRS-shaped hole in the bottom.

Later on, I'll tell you about my SMART Kai-Zen plan that provides income to me, tax-free, and ensures the remaining balance is transferred tax-free to my family when I'm gone.

THE BENEFITS OF TAX AWARENESS AND ACTUARIAL ARBITRAGE

Like tax-aware arbitrage, actuarial arbitrage is really about where to put your money to get the most benefit. We all want to get the most benefit from what is ours and to take profitable advantage of all the different options available to us with as little risk as possible. No risk is even better.

Imagine if you could buy an FDIC-insured CD today with a 12 percent interest rate. You would—we all would. A 12 percent risk-free return is a YES! Even better, if you could get that 12 percent CD into a Roth IRA, then you could take tax-free income or accumulate your account value ... all without future tax liabilities.

We naturally want the option that provides the most financial benefit. Let's make up an example to illustrate this concept. Assume you're planning on putting a large sum of money into the bank. Over the next ten years, you intend to take all of your principal out of the account as your first bucket of money in retirement. After ten years, you know that none of the money you originally deposited will remain, just whatever interest you've earned along the way.

Now, you have the option of putting your money into one of two banks. The first, *Bank of Normal*, offers you the following: 3 percent on your deposited amount and permission to take out one-tenth of your money each year without any early withdrawal penalties. This is not a bad offer, considering the low interest rates we currently have and some liquidity without an early withdrawal penalty.

Thankfully, you check in with the other bank, the *Friendly Bank*. They are so friendly, it's hard to believe. What they offer astounds you: you can earn interest when the economy is good and you can never lose any money if the economy turns sour. You'll pay no fees on your deposits, so the only time your account goes down in value is when you take money out of the account. You can access your money, same as the Normal Bank, but after the tenth year, because you've been so kind to trust them with your hard-earned money, Friendly Bank will actually pay you a pension for your entire life! Wow, that's pretty friendly, isn't it? Even better, if you are married, you can make it a joint life pension so not only will it benefit you but it can also benefit your spouse. And, if the economy is good, you get "pension credits" and your monthly payout will rise the longer you delay taking it. Once they start your pension payout, they guarantee they'll never reduce or take it away, even if you have a $0 balance in their bank.

It's kind of a no-brainer that the Friendly Bank is just a better deal. Now, there's no Friendly Bank, but what I've described for you is an annuity product that is used in a way by SMART Advisor Network members that differs from how most advisors use it, resulting in a unique outcome that favors our clientele.

These products come and go, but when SMART Advisor Network members find a product that can be actuarially configured to provide an advantage of mortality credits to our clientele, we are swift about taking appropriately sized positions in them so the actuarial and tax-diversification profits can accrue and work toward our client's long-term planning goals and objectives while minimizing, eliminating, or shifting as much risk as possible onto the issuer of the account and away from our client.

When you understand how to mix actuarial arbitrage with tax awareness, you end up with a very SMART Retirement plan—one that affords you the advantage of the Strategic Movement Around Retirement Taxation® as well as the earning potential created by actuarial float.

I'd like to stress that SMART plans add the concepts of float, actuarial arbitrage, and tax awareness to traditional planning. But it's these small changes in your planning that open the door to a more tax-diversified retirement, resulting in more income and less tax!

Financial institutions and insurance companies do not operate without financial risk. The long-term promises carry inherent counterparty risk. So are ratings and regulators not enough? SMART Advisor Network forensic accountant Tom Gober explains that it's a matter of transparency. Together we developed the TSR% ratio. It's a fact-based approach to assessing financial risk that's easy to understand and more meaningful than ratings. Gober is the go-to guy for plaintiffs, lawyers, and law enforcement fighting insurance fraud. He joined the SMART Advisor Network to start a proactive movement to protect policyholders.

To see a sample of our TSR% report, please turn to the appendix.

CHAPTER 4

GET SMART: ENJOY THE STRATEGIC MOVEMENT AROUND RETIREMENT TAXATION®

When I first got into this business twenty-five years ago, I was taught—and believed—that the worst place you could possibly be invested was in a taxable account. Why pay taxes when there appeared to be better options? After all, with a traditional IRA and 401(k) account, we can defer the tax into the future and we'll probably pay less. I also believed that the best place in the world we could be was in a tax-free account.

But, of course, the yields sometimes aren't attractive enough in tax-free accounts (especially back before 1997 when Roth IRAs became available), so I believed that ideally, a well-rounded retirement strategy should have some taxable, tax-deferred, and tax-free holdings. Either way, I was dedicated in my belief that the worst place of those three options was always a taxable account and paying tax now.

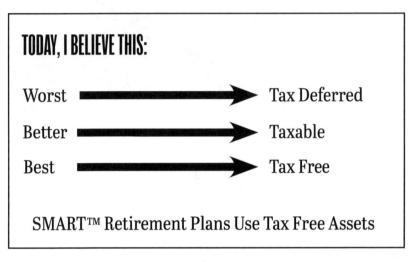

Fig. 23

Well, today I believe this: the worst place in the world you can be overinvested is in a tax-deferred account.

I'll give you a minute to catch your breath because I know that comes as a shock to many of you, considering that the most popular retirement savings vehicle in America is, by far, the company-sponsored, pretax 401(k) plan.

Consider this: If tax rates go up significantly, many of us won't be able to out-earn the negative tax effects without taking considerable added risk. That means it's possible that the balance of your IRA, 401(k), and other retirement accounts today is the most these accounts may ever be worth on a net tax-adjusted basis.

You see, as taxes increase, your pretax account net value goes down because you're essentially exposing these dollars (a.k.a. your future retirement income) to paying higher tax rates. That's why it's quite possible that it's better to pay the tax now, when we know what we have to pay—especially since we're at historically low tax rates.

I believe, as many of you do, that taxes are going to go up, which means if we pay taxes now, we'll actually be paying at a discount compared to what we will likely pay in the future.

What's good for *us* isn't in the best interests of the tax authorities. I like how economist and fellow *Forbes* contributor Leonard Burman said it: "[T]he government is bringing in more now, but giving up much more in the future."[16]

With the recent passing of the SECURE Act and resultant requirement for certain nonspousal beneficiaries to take their inherited funds out of the IRA within ten years, beneficiaries will quickly begin paying higher income tax rates on their inherited IRAs and 401(k) accounts.

At the SMART Advisor Network, all of our planning is focused on paying the lowest possible effective tax cost. Today, advisors all over the United States fight each other to earn business from affluent Americans to help them manage their money. Their marketing message to these financially well-off prospective clients is, "We will help you earn more!" That message is not one I share, because I personally do not believe in fee-based money management.

When you look at the lifetime earnings statistics that you can find within the Bureau of Labor Statistics Consumer Expenditure Surveys, you'll find that the average American can expect their lifetime income to be distributed as follows (and I am taking some data consolidation and mathematical rounding liberty here):

- 40% to satisfy some form of tax: income tax, payroll tax, sales tax, property tax, tax on utilities—the list goes on

- 25% on debt payments: mortgages, cars, school loans, credit cards, etc.

---

16   https://www.forbes.com/sites/deborahljacobs/2012/03/26/why-and-how-congress-should-curb-roth-iras/#53eae67a17f8

- 25% to supporting our lifestyle: buying clothes, food, entertainment, etc. (i.e., the good parts of life)

- 10% to savings

Obviously, over time as debts get paid, the savings rate tends to rise, but 10 percent is the lifetime average. So savings tend to be back-loaded in the later working years. But money saved early during youth has more time to compound and grow, which means that later start date inhibits growth potential since the funds have less time to compound.

Also, these are today's numbers. For future generations, the disparity between what's spent on lifestyle expenses and savings versus debt may get skewed. In this FOMO-filled (Fear Of Missing Out), social-media-fueled society, mature affluent retirees and those approaching retirement fear their hard-earned money will go to adult "children" who do not possess the financial discipline to manage the inheritance. More than once in discussions about tax-motivated gifting programs, I've heard: "I don't want to throw my hard-earned money at their poor spending habits" (if this sounds like you, our SMART Debt Free 4 Life Gifting program teaches children and grandchildren how to be responsible with money and eliminate debt and accumulate cash for their future.).

Advisors focus on that last piece of the financial puzzle, touting their ability to help you earn more on the 10 percent you save. To me, it makes the most sense to focus on the "big" numbers that heavily affect our lifetime financial well-being: taxes and debt. If we strategically plan to reduce tax and/or debt burden, naturally the savings rate rises.

But when it comes to the management of that accumulated 10 percent, the question remains: Which assets are "best"? Well, tax-free is still not a stand-alone solution. Why? I've owned tax-free bonds in the past, and the bond broker told me they'd be income tax-free, and they were. But they weren't free from the alternative minimum tax, which turned my tax-free bonds into taxable bonds.

So what is the best option? Truly tax-free is the winner. When you can find a way of creating income without any tax ramifications, it is the only way to create completely tax-free income. The key to a SMART Retirement plan is to lower your effective tax cost to its lowest potential by mixing pretax, taxable, and tax-free assets intelligently. Now let's talk about how that's done.

The big fallacy everyone has been told is that they will be in a lower tax bracket in retirement. Guess what? That's not what we're seeing now, and here's why. When you're young or middle-aged and working, you have a lot of different deductions. You may be able to deduct the interest on your house payments, exemptions for student loan interest, exemptions for dependent children who live with you, deductions and credits for retirement plan contributions, health coverage, and so on. And while retirees may have given charities monetary donations while they were working, now they give time. And time is not a deductible expense.

So what's left for seniors to deduct? Normally, these days, just the standard deduction. This is why most of the clients who were told they'd be in a lower tax bracket in retirement have found that they are not in a lower tax bracket after all.

SMART BOARD

The Myth of the Lowered Postretirement Tax Bracket

You may be in a HIGHER tax bracket in retirement because you lose:

1. Mortgage interest deductions
2. At-home child exemptions
3. Retirement plan contributions
4. Charitable giving
5. Student loan interest
6. Flex accounts and HSAs

And you gain:

1. Uncontrolled required minimum distributions

What's left? Your standard deductions.
Do you believe tax rates are going up?

Fig. 24

SMART POINT

The SMART Retirement planning strategy revolves around the strategic movement around retirement taxes. That means you have to dig deeper than simply believing the old adage that retired people pay less in taxes in their retirement. Remember, your allowable deductions and credits are going to go down significantly when you're retired because chances are you will lose:

- **Dependents**: It's doubtful that you'll still have underage children to support while you're in retirement. You'll also lose all the associated tax breaks, such as those for childcare.

- **Mortgage interest**: It's never a good idea to head into retirement with debt, which likely means your home will be paid off before you leave the workforce. Plus, as you age and pay down your principal, your mortgage interest expenses will drop dramatically, thereby decreasing your deduction. Lastly, state and local tax write-offs are now capped at $10,000.

- **Student loan interest**: Your student loans will also hopefully be paid off by the time you reach retirement, so no longer will you have that interest deduction to write off.

- **Retirement plan contributions**: You won't be contributing to retirement accounts when you no longer have an earned income.

- **Charitable giving**: Most retirees switch from donating money to donating time once they leave the workforce. Time is an amazing gift, but it's not tax deductible.

- **Flex accounts and HSAs**: As a retiree on Medicare, you won't have use for HSAs anymore and you'll have no employer offering a flex account, so you'll lose that excluded contribution. Worse, you may even begin taking qualified distributions from your HSA, which can increase your provisional income.

But it's not all loss. You also gain something … even if you don't want to:

- **Uncontrolled required minimum distributions**: The least thought-of source of taxation in retirement is the required minimum distributions (RMDs) a retiree must begin taking from their 401(k), Traditional IRA, or other pretax retirement plan once they reach age seventy-two. These distributions are based on a formula developed to force money out of the account over the retiree's lifetime. As the retiree ages, the government's distribution divisor reduces, requiring a higher percentage of the prior year's year-end balance to be distributed, often making it difficult to manage the retiree's resulting tax bracket in retirement. This is especially true of IRA and 401(k) accounts of substantial value.

At the time the third edition of *SMART Retirement* was released, Joe Biden had just started his first year in office. At that point, he was focused on pushing through another large COVID relief bill ... so even though Trump lowered tax rates during his presidency, it's easy to see that this administration will be taking a different approach. And likely creating enough new debt that the next administration will have little room to consider any tax reduction.

Even if we had an administration that was focused on lowering tax rates, I would still expect rising taxes because when I refer to higher tax rates, I'm talking about the imminent possibility of them rising over the whole of your retirement.

If you are fifty years old, for example, and you have fifteen years before retirement and then another twenty to thirty years to enjoy retirement, that's as many as forty-five years that taxes will be adjusting. Do you think you can count on every incoming administration to keep taxes low for the next forty-five years? I sure don't! In recent years, we've seen an influx of congresspeople like Alexandria Ocasio-Cortez giving support to taxing high-income earners at rates up to 70 percent, and other fresh, young politicians have voiced similar preferences, while senior senators such as Elizabeth Warren and Bernie Sanders favor additional taxes on wealth.

If this represents the political sentiment of the future, then it's even more important and advantageous to create your SMART plan today. That way, if there are any tax con-sequences from Roth conversions, funding the 10-pay policy, or from funding your company-sponsored Roth 401(k), you can pay taxes a single time, while tax rates are low, and gain full ownership of your money. With proper repositioning of your retirement assets, you can plan today to never pay taxes on those same funds again.

And let's just say that history doesn't repeat itself and we do, by some miracle, end up enjoying low tax rates for the next half-century. Taxes are taxes—no matter how low they are. They still take money out of your pocket and put it in someone else's, thus it's worth attempting to eliminate them now. Plus, the compound wealth will all be tax-free.

THE FIRST STEP TO DESIGNING A SMART RETIREMENT PLAN

Match your deductions and exemptions to your retirement plan distributions

Standard deductions*	$12,400
Spousal deduction	<u>$12,400</u>
	$24,800

*For 2020, under 65

Fig. 25

The first step in designing a truly SMART Retirement plan is to be aware of your deduction. The standard deduction as of 2020 for those under 65 is $24,800 for married couples and $12,400 for single filers. For couples who are both 65 or older, the standard deduction increases, bringing it to $27,400 for married couples and $14,050 for single filers.

This is important to know because if you are married and take out $24,800 ($27,400 if married and both over 65) or less each year from your retirement plan (IRAs or 401(k)s), you'll pay no tax. Sometimes when I teach these strategies to build wealth by being more tax savvy, advisors want to take this to the "tax-free" extreme and vilify all tax-deferred assets.

But a SMART plan is all about balance. If you don't have a monthly defined pension benefit, and your retirement income will come solely from an IRA and/or 401(k), you are better off taking that $24,800/$27,400 or less out a year and ultimately use that to offset your standard deduction, resulting in a tax-free, completely spendable distribution from your retirement plan. If you need more income than Social Security and $24,800/$27,400 from your IRA and/or 401(k), don't worry—we have more SMART techniques to deploy, which we'll talk about in the next chapter.

So why aren't advisors really educating the public about matching deductions to retirement-plan-sourced income? Perhaps they don't know or don't want to be perceived as giving tax advice. Either way, it's important for you to be tax aware in your retirement planning.

Standard deductions is the term describing the amount that all taxpayers who don't itemize are permitted to deduct from their gross income so they have some amount of income that is protected from taxes. Since seniors lose out on many deductions (like the mortgage interest and charitable contributions), they will generally take the standard deduction because it's larger than the expenses they can legally include in an itemization.

The standard deduction varies depending on your filing and marital status and it can be slightly larger for widows and widowers or those with certain visual impairments. And even if a senior were to maintain their itemized deductions under the old law, TaxFoundation.org reports that the Tax Cuts and Jobs Act reduced the number of itemized filers by 28.5 million households.

One big problem with 401(k)s and IRAs is provisional income. Provisional income is the calculation that's used to determine how much of your Social Security income is taxable. To really understand this concept, let's talk about Bill and Sally.

PROBLEM WITH 401K + IRAS: PROVISIONAL INCOME!

Provisional income example – Bill & Sally

50% of SS benefit	$30,000 x ½	=	$15,000
Annual distribution from IRA		=	$55,000
Provisional income for SS tax purposes:			$70,000
At $70,000 prov. income, 85% of SS taxed			
85% x 30,000 = $25,500 @ 12% tax		=	$3,060 Tax on SS!
Total taxable income		=	$55,400
[$55,000 IRA + $25,500 SS – deductions ($24,800)]			
Tax on $55,400 taxable income		=	$3,339
Total **tax** due on actual income of **$85,000**		=	$6,253

For 2020, couple under 65

Fig. 26

Bill and Sally take home $30,000[17] a year in Social Security benefits and $4,583 collectively per month in distributions from their IRAs. This gives them a total income of $85,000. Provisional income is determined by taking 50 percent of a retiree's Social Security benefit and adding it to their other sources of taxable income. The sum is then compared to IRS-published tables (shown in figures 27 and 28) and the taxable amount is determined. For Bill and Sally, that means that $15,000 of their Social Security income is added into this calculation along with the full $55,000 taken from their IRAs.

---

17   "Income from Social Security," Pension Rights Center, http://www.pensionrights.org/publications/statistic/income-social-security.

When you consider these two together for this calculation, the provisional income for determining Social Security taxation for Bill and Sally is $70,000. With $70,000 of provisional income, 85 percent of their Social Security will be taxed. Thus, you take 85 percent of their *total* $30,000 in Social Security income, and that equals $25,500 that they have to claim as taxable income on a benefit that was originally meant to be tax-free.

Let's assume that they're in a 12 percent tax bracket, which means they'll owe $3,060 in tax just on their Social Security income, which—again—was always intended to be a tax-free benefit. But that's only part of the story. Since they're also taking distributions from their IRA, their actual total taxable income is $55,400. At a 10 percent tax rate, that means they'll owe another $3,339 in taxes on that IRA income, bringing their annual tax bill up to around $6,253. That's a lot—especially if their spending burden is amplified due to increases in their Medicare supplemental health insurance premiums.

You might have found those last few sentences confusing. I understand why; seriously, are Bill and Sally in a 10 percent tax bracket or a 12 percent tax bracket? Well … both, actually.

You see, our income tax system is progressive and multidimensional so the first $19,400 of earnings above the standard deduction are in the 10 percent bracket and income over that crosses over into the 12 percent federal tax bracket. With a progressive tax system, the tax calculations aren't based simply on the flat rates of each tax bracket. Without Social Security included, the average tax rate is 10.8 percent, but with Social Security included, the actual tax rate becomes 11.3 percent.

Now, before we try to solve Bill and Sally's problem, I'd like to stop here for a moment and take a look at this. Is the answer here getting a higher rate of return or is it about being smarter about what's taxable and what's not taxable? Is it a smarter approach to figure out how to reposition our sources of income using a more tax-aware approach to create a better result?

I'm going to show you that this is exactly the case for Bill and Sally, and many American retirees just like them, but first, let's take a look at a few charts that you need to know.

Married couples	% of SS taxed
Under $32,000	0%
$32,000 - $44,000	50%
Over $44,000	85%

Fig. 27

If you're a debt-free married couple and your lifestyle needs are frugal, you want to strive, when possible, to keep your provisional income under $32,000 because that will ensure that none of your Social Security income is taxable. Remember: this is not your full potential retirement income. You could receive $1 million in tax-free income and have a $0 provisional income.

If your provisional income is between $32,000 and $44,000, 50 percent of that Social Security income is included in your income tax calculation. If it's over $44,000, then 85 percent of your Social Security income is included in the income tax calculation. These are numbers that you need to know if you want to target your lowest potential tax rate.

But remember—targeting the lowest potential rate doesn't mean that's all you earn. It's just about controlling what's taxable and reportable and what's not. A person receiving $80,000 per year from their Roth 401(k) or Roth IRA and/or a portion from cash-value life insurance would register at $0 for the Social Security provisional income tax thresholds. In this way, a SMART plan focuses on limiting your postretirement taxes—not your postretirement income. Done properly, SMART planning increases income on a net, after-tax basis.

Single & widowers	% of SS taxed
Under $25,000	0%
$25,000 - $34,000	50%
Over $34,000	85%

Fig. 28

If you're single or widowed, these numbers are lower. If your income is under $25,000, then your Social Security isn't included in your tax calculation. If your provisional income is $25,000 to $34,000, then up to 50 percent of your Social Security is tax-calculated at a graduated amount. If your provisional income is more than $34,000, then up to 85 percent of your Social Security income will be tax-calculated.

Let's go back to Bill and Sally and help them get SMART. First, we want to move some money out of the IRA into a Roth and possibly other tax-free assets. That way, they can take just $20,000 in taxable income from the IRA and $35,000 in tax-free income from the Roth and other tax-free assets to get that full $55,000. But for the provisional income calculation, the only thing we would include is 50 percent of their Social Security ($15,000) and the taxable IRA distribution of $20,000, giving us a total provisional income of $35,000, which is over the $32,000 limit for married couples, making $1,500 of their Social Security income taxable. However, because they get a standard deduction of $25,100, the amount of total tax due would be zero.

Because tax-free income is just that—free from taxation—we have zero tax on their $30,000 Social Security income and we've also got zero tax on the $35,000 of tax-free income, which means the only reportable taxable income becomes $1,500 from Social Security and the amount that is being distributed from their IRA, which is $20,000. And for a married couple with $21,500 of income, the standard deduction will bring their total taxable income to $0.

FIXING BILL AND SALLY

Move some money away from IRA to tax-exempt assets

50% of SS benefit **$30,000** x ½	=	**$15,000**
Annual distribution from IRA	=	**$20,000**
Tax-free income	=	**$35,000**
Provisional income for SS tax purposes:		**$35,000**
Provisional income	=	**$35,000**
$1,500 SS taxable + $20,000 IRA income	=	**$21,500**
− $24,800 standard deduction		
Total tax due on $70,000 income	=	**$0**

Fig. 29

So you can see where getting Bill and Sally SMART over time will provide a much better net-spendable income for them in retirement, instead of the traditional planning methods. And while there will be taxes along the way to get there, they will be paid just once. If they're paid soon, these taxes will be paid at what are likely some of the lowest tax rates in our nation's history. Better yet, if the plan is set up properly, the money that SMART saves them in taxes will continue to compound; whatever's left will ultimately be inherited by their family—completely tax-free.

FROM THE SMART WHYS TO THE SMART HOWS

So how do we do this? We want to be smart about funding a SMART plan to add to our traditional planning. The Roth IRA is one of the great financial wonders of the world, but there are some limitations surrounding who can fund a Roth.

These are the numbers for 2021: For married couples, the phaseout starts at $198,000 and ineligibility at $208,000. For singles, the phaseout begins at $125,000 and ineligibility is at $140,000. For those of you who are working toward retirement with income that falls below these limits, the Roth is a strong option for you.

What options do you have if you're married with an income over $208,000, or single with an income over $140,000? You may want to consider a backdoor approach by funding a nondeductible IRA. There are two different ways you can go about this. First, you can fund a nondeductible IRA and then convert it to a Roth. But your best option is to work with your employer and ask them to add a Roth 401(k) option to your company plan, if it doesn't currently offer one.

 If you are a business owner or a solo entrepreneur, such as a realtor, consultant, or online marketer, are paid by 1099 (even if you have W-2 income elsewhere), have a cash-heavy business, or a small business with minimal or no employees, I HIGHLY recommend you consult your SMART Advisor Network advisor to discuss SMART plans.

They will help you structure a very unique Roth-based plan that you can fund with contributions of up to $62,000* per year. These contributions are not restricted by income-funding limitations like a SEP IRA would be, and 100 percent of your income can be allocated to the plan. Married solo entrepreneurs may be eligible to fund an additional $62,000 per year for their spouse (slightly less when under 50). More on my own personal SMART Planz 401(k) in Chapter 6.

*Funding limits apply and subject to actuarial guidelines.

Roth conversions can sometimes be tricky and taxing. Additional guidance from a member of our SMART Advisor Network is highly advisable. These tax-aware planners can gain access to tax-planning experts like tax attorney Rick Law and his law partner, Zach Hesselbaum, LLM, who can further advise. When needed, SMART Advisors can help you get detailed tax analysis from highly regarded experts like Stephen Biggie, CPA, a partner at the nationally recognized tax advisory and CPA firm Keebler & Associates.

Plus, for business owners, your SMART Advisor has exclusive access to the SMART Planz, LLC CEO and chief actuary Brad Barlow. Brad is a top-level actuary with twenty-seven years' experience and is a fellow of the Society of Actuaries with an advanced degree in mathematics from Ohio State.

The next question is: How much should you fund or convert to Roth? The internet can be a helpful resource in many respects, but it's also limiting if you don't know what you're looking for or how to locate it. One way we see this over and over is in the prevalence of retirement calculators dotting the web landscape. These calculators claim to help users determine how much money they will need during retirement based on their anticipated expenses and, thus, how much they need to save at their anticipated average rate of return.

Sadly, these calculators (and really, the whole approach of anticipating full future retirement income needs and focusing on how much to save) are lacking for several reasons.

First, the Social Security numbers used by calculators are based on pure assumption and don't consider many of the problems facing Social Security, as well as the very real possibility of future benefit rollbacks to compensate for the dropping ratio of workers to recipients.

In addition, these calculators may assume that your returns will average out. They neglect to show the effects of market fluctuations, and the market will fluctuate. These calculators have no way of anticipating how wildly the markets will fluctuate or in what years you might see no return or negative returns. This can be an extreme problem, as you saw illustrated in Chapter 2.

A third problem with these generic calculators is that they don't recalculate based on how your tax situation will change as you age. They may not account for the losses in deductions you'll experience or the effects of your UNcontrolled required minimum distributions that will grow over time.

With WHERE AM **I AT**™, we first focus on the I, which stands for your Income. Although income can be hard to target using Monte Carlo-simulation online calculators, we should have a goal of achieving our current net income after we retire. Few people, if any, have ever said, "Wow, it will be great to retire on 75 percent of what I make today." Although Wall Street has approached retirement planning with this discounted lifestyle mindset for decades, it's wrong and unnecessary.

Instead, a better way is to look at your NET income, i.e., what you deposit from your net paycheck (if you're still working) or from the sum of your monthly distributions (if you're retired) into your bank account each and every month. That is the target. From that income target, we first deduct your expected Social Security. Although the future financial stability of Social Security is in question, we need to account for how it offsets what we need to take from our retirement savings to meet our net-income objective.

The most senior and successful SMART Advisor Network members have direct access to Heather Schreiber, RICP, who is regarded as a national expert on Social Security claiming optimization. She is often called in to clarify misinformation people have gotten from advisors who try to get prospects at free Social Security events.

Next, we look at the **AT** portion of the equation. If you're a fortunate person who will receive a defined benefit monthly pension check, deduct that as well from what you need to take from your retirement **A**ssets. What's left is what will be needed from your retirement assets to make up the difference from your working income. Now, how do we get to that number?

First, let's seek to simply match our IRA and 401(k) distribution amounts to the standard deduction, which is increasing over time. Consider into your calculations income coming to you from a defined benefit plan that may fully offset your standard deduction. Anything that's over that amount, ideally we want to distribute from a Roth or another tax-exempt resource when possible.

But be careful when making Roth conversions! Be aware of any excessive provisional income the conversion triggers, making a large percentage of your Social Security taxable and potentially increasing your Medicare premium. This is why it's always a good idea to get help from a SMART Advisor before you do any conversions to avoid being excessively taxed on the Roth conversion of your existing IRA balances. Plus, for higher-net-worth clients and HENRYs, Roth may not be the best tax-free plan.

ALWAYS REMEMBER:

Where am …

I	AT
Income **A**sset	**A**sset Value after **T**ax

WHERE SHOULD YOU INVEST YOUR MONEY?

The inference here is that finding the right investment for your money in a pursuit to accumulate more is the key to ensuring your retirement security. Too many people think that the accumulation phase of retirement, which would be a lot like the phase of mountain climbing where you're hoisting yourself up the side of a cliff in an attempt to reach the summit, is the most important phase. But as I said earlier, the descent is the more dangerous part of the climbing excursion. It's also the most important—because every mountain climber wants to make it back home safely.

Planning only for your retirement as if it were all based on the principles of accumulation is like planning for a mountain-climbing trip by only prepping for the rise up the mountain, and having no clue how you're going to safely get back down. If you want to succeed, then you have to pack your retirement-planning bags accordingly for both your retirement ascent and eventual descent.

When it comes to retirement planning, your actual retirement—those years when you're taking consistent distributions from your savings—that's the climb down the mountain. If you think about it, that's actually what all the prep was for. That is the stage of your retirement that determines the success or failure of your planning, and that's the place where you want to be sure you've made the best decisions.

Every year, close to a thousand highly trained, experienced, and prepared mountain climbers try to scale Everest, one of the world's tallest peaks. Only about half make it to the top. Do you think the hundreds of climbers who don't make it to the top are turning around by choice? Or do you think that at some point, when they realize they can't make it to the summit, their safe descent becomes their top priority?

Tragedy strikes when the unwise climber decides to continue on the current path without regard for their safe descent. Sometimes, this is due to conditions beyond their control; many other times it's their own miscalculations. The parallels are easy to see here to retirement planning, where being too aggressive or too optimistic at the wrong time can lead to potentially bad outcomes.

Plus, far too many people these days approach the descent into retirement with "extra weight" packed into their backpacks in the form of debt. Debt in retirement improperly allocates your resources and compounds wealth and creates income for your lender rather than doing so for you.

So asking where you should put your money, and then leaving it at that, is like looking at the maps and topography, talking to other climbers, and working with Sherpas solely for the goal of reaching the top of Everest and then having no plan, equipment, or method for getting back down. SMART planning requires monitoring, recalculations, and modifications as times, tax rates, and overall market, economic, and political conditions change.

I find that time, math, and money rarely move in the same direction. It is quite strange because the whole idea of compounding interest and capital appreciation are based on a rate of return compounded over time. In fact, the math for appreciation is based on four variables: present value, future value, rate of return, and time.

It follows, then, that time, money, and math should be aligned and earning more income for retirees and pre-retirees—right? Well, maybe. If you take risks with your money, values can go up—but they can also go down. Market historians and verified data offer long-term rates of return that are very attractive, yet when the economy gets rough, money can be (and has been) lost, which doesn't help folks and their families grow toward a stronger financial future.

When modeling your retirement, it's important to discount the accuracy of averages and Monte Carlo-based calculations. Your best guide is history and understanding that cycles repeat. Then you have to factor in the negative effect of taxes compounding over time. Beyond that, there are even more threats to your income and a greater chance to lose money—that is, unless you are SMART when planning and work toward minimizing your future tax liabilities over time with realistic assumptions on income and growth potential, with a historical basis for relying on your assumptions.

What else can you do to help stay on the right track regardless of how time and markets work to erode your money? You can start by diversifying among many different types of assets. Avoid biases such as, "I only invest in mutual funds," or, "Just stocks and bonds." Also, don't build in a bias toward products you may not understand, such as, "I don't believe in insurance products like life insurance or annuities." Allow yourself to be open to all possibilities—they all may have merit in a well-designed and truly diversified plan.

Next, you should not try to time market conditions. Instead, build a great plan based on sound principles and then stick with it. Allow time and your money to work for you and do not allow your emotions to work against you and your money.

Lastly, make sure you regularly review your plan. Keep track of where you are, what you have, and where you want your retirement planning to go. The ultimate key is to utilize time and achieve planning success methodically with SMART math.

To really understand the danger of the average rate of return–based mindset, play our game at: www.SecureIncome4Life.com. It's eye-opening!

THE MORAL OF THE STORY

I'm not saying or trying to imply that the question of what to invest in isn't worth asking or answering. It can be a meaningful part of your retirement planning. Focusing exclusively on investments, however, doesn't allow you to get a full picture of everything involved in designing a truly SMART Retirement. One that creates a stable, tax-efficient, lifetime income that adjusts to inflation. In a later chapter, I'll show you exactly what I personally own, what I do with my own money, and why.

Inflation is something that's going to hurt us all. The budget you make now for your planned retirement spending is fine, except for just one thing: you don't have any idea how much everything will actually cost once you retire. On average, we can expect inflation to raise the cost of goods and services by 3.22 percent a year. But, like fluctuating returns, inflation rates vary, such as in

1990 when inflation averaged 5.4 percent, or in 1974 when inflation averaged 11 percent.[18]

If you retire during or after a period of excessive inflation, you might deplete your savings far quicker if your market-linked investments cannot keep pace. What certainly can help is enhancing your retirement nest egg with better tax management.

It's also worth considering the fact that inflation is a multidimensional thing. It's not just an increase in prices. Most Americans would agree that their view of inflation has to do with the prices of certain items. If the prices of those items they buy most frequently are up from the prior year, then they know they are dealing with the effects of inflation.

But the other concern we need to think about is monetary inflation, which is a whole different type of inflation. It is a simple inflation to track because it means the government is asking the Federal Reserve to print more money. They are asking to inflate the amount of money available.

Modern monetary inflation started during the Kennedy administration and has been a steady policy in Washington since it began, regardless of political party. Democrats have inflated the money supply just as the Republicans have inflated the money supply.

And you know what? We, as Americans, like it. More money around equals the feeling of greater prosperity … as long as the money holds its value. Yet with close

---

18   Bureau of Labor Statistics, "CPI Inflation Calculator," https://www.bls.gov/data/inflation_calcula-tor.htm.

to $4 trillion added to the money supply since 2008, it's possible that it won't.[19]

Monetary inflation played a key role in the decision to abandon the gold standard in the US on August 15, 1971, leading to the "Nixon Shock." In essence, the change to a floating exchange rate represented a form of reset for our own currency right here in the United States.

Price inflation hurts us most while in retirement because most retirees live off a fixed income, so it is especially painful if the interest rates available from safe investments and bank-offered savings plans are low. It is a classic case of "costs are up and revenue is flat."

However, there is a lot more to it once you also factor in the dangers of monetary inflation. We each need to ask ourselves and our advisors what's being done with our finances to manage that possibility. One of the best moves we can make is to add actuarial-based products with floating interest rates and a "floor" minimum rate today. Using mortality credit is the smartest thing to add to your planning, and SMART Advisors know exactly how to do that for you.

---

19   Mike Patton, "Why Inflation Is Low, Despite the Fed's Massive Monetary Expansion," *Forbes*, December 28, 2015, http://www.forbes.com/sites/mikepatton/2015/12/28/why-inflation-is-low-despite-the-feds-massive-monetary-expansion/.

CHAPTER 5
SMART PEOPLE, SMART PLANS

For many people, the income available when sticking to the standard deductions simply isn't enough to live the lifestyle they want to lead based on the wealth they've accumulated. Of course, after reading this book, you're probably starting to see that trying to take more out of your tax-qualified, pretax retirement plans may provide you with increased income, but at the cost of an ever-rising tax liability. Let's take a look beyond the Roth to a hundred-plus-year-old product that banks and billionaires seem to favor: high cash value, low death benefit life insurance—specifically, for me, 10-pay.

HIGHER INCOME WITHOUT TAXATION

A 10-payment or shorter life insurance payment period (often referred to as a limited-pay life insurance policy) offers a lifetime of policy benefits after a limited period of premium deposits. Your SMART Advisor may recommend different types for you based on your unique circumstances, including indexed universal life, whole life, or both. I personally own both.

Depending on the type of coverage you choose, the policy can simply stay in force on a paid-up basis after the premium payments are made. While the payments are stretched over a certain term, this is not a term life policy—it's a high cash value, low death benefit policy offering a lifetime of benefits to you. That means that the death benefits are payable even if the insured passes away thirty years after they stopped making premium payments. It also means that the policy accrues significant cash values.

The enhancement of cash value is a function of "overfunding." This added cash grows and is available to you faster as paid-up additions, giving you access to cash that you can—no, that you should—use to make major purchases, replacing ALL forms of bank financing. The cash is ultimately available to distribute to you in your retirement via tax-free withdrawals or tax-free structured loans. And, since it's classified as either return of your basis or a loan, it's received without income taxation.

If you have debts, the lifetime access at any age helps you avoid using credit cards, auto financing, and mortgages with their expensive interest rates, essentially becoming debt-free for life—financing your own residence, vacation homes, and business liabilities without the tricky amortization math used by traditional lenders hurting you financially. Instead, the interest will now be continuously compounding for YOU rather than THEM!

WHY CONSIDER HIGH CASH VALUE LIFE INSURANCE FOR A PORTION OF YOUR TAX-FREE ASSETS OUTSIDE THE ROTH?

→ *Cash accumulated is accessible as tax-preferred income at any age*
→ *No contribution limits*
→ *No income cap limitation*
→ *No provisional income*
→ *Safe harbor for legislative change ('82, '84, '88)*
→ *Benefits paid to family are tax-preferred*
→ *Waiver of contributions if disabled*
→ *Benefits for chronic care and terminal illness*

Fig. 30

If you are 100 percent debt-free and have been for years, you may still have concerns about your children and grandchildren's debts and/or spending habits, which is consistent with the way our financially well-off clients generally feel. Today, social media advertisers, merchants, and credit card companies have made debt addiction a true disability. SMART Advisor Network members are focused not only on increasing your tax-adjusted wealth but also helping your children and grandchildren develop a SMART approach to cash management, breaking the financially devastating effects of impulsively buying on credit.

You might be wondering why I'm talking about 10-pay insurance after bringing up the issue of debt management and income shortages for retirees. Here's the thing: With the right high cash value, low death benefit policy in force, you'll be accruing significant cash that you can access before and after you've retired. That accumulated cash is always available to you and when you take it out, you can do so without tax ramifications. It isn't counted as provisional income, so it doesn't offset your Social Security and trigger taxation. It is in no way taxable nor does it count in calculating your Medicare premium.

There are also no contribution limits to a 10-pay policy other than your ability to afford making the scheduled premiums, which is easy if you "dollar-cost average" a less tax-efficient asset into the limited-pay, high cash value insurance over a period of time. There is no income limitation, no required minimum distribution, and no conversion required.

Ultimately, what I'm saying is that with a 10-pay life insurance policy, you never have to worry about the income you take out, because it's not going to trigger a tax if you keep the contract in force. There is simply no 1099 or other tax reporting. As such, you'll enjoy Roth-like benefits from a different tax-free asset.

The most beneficial, high cash value policies have changed and evolved over time. The tax benefits are firmly rooted in the tax code and changes have always been grandfathered, honoring prior law arrangements. Tax law changes around this class of product happened in 1982, 1984, and 1988 with prior law prevailing. A lot of what we're going to show you today was even more readily available, with bigger amounts of early funding allowed and faster tax-free benefits in the past. Ironically, the recent passage of the COVID-19 relief bill made the greatest change to the life insurance business in the last thirty-five years.

Section 7702 was actuarially altered in a way that will significantly financially favor the amount of cash that can be stored and grown inside a life insurance policy. This massive tax policy change is uniquely timed as Washington insiders transition from public service back to the private sector.

Here's why I prefer smartly designed life insurance over other tax-free options:

- Income from high cash value policies can be completely tax-free.

- Death benefits paid to your family who inherit it when you're gone are completely tax-free.

- Certain contribution limits may increase when purchasing life insurance through pension plans, such as the SMART Planz 401(k) and the SMART 401(k) with an added defined benefit plan.

- There are riders, such as a waiver of premium for disability, that can allow premiums to be waived in the event of a disability.

- There are benefits for chronic care and terminal illness so you can leverage your policy benefits for those uncomfortable and unwelcome life realities.

You know, these things happen. Disability and long-term care and chronic illness are real-life incidents. This is a product that has leveraged benefits for those unpleasant eventualities. Those are just some of the reasons I heavily fund, use, and own a 10-pay for myself as a way to build tax-exempt assets and to have the death benefit to pay future taxes to convert any tax-deferred assets I have remaining into a Roth IRA or after-tax asset when I die.

So, beyond the tax-advantaged lifetime access, my 10-pay also benefits me when I need to make major purchases and take future supplemental retirement income. Simultaneously, the eventual death benefit plays a major role in my long-term, tax-aware approach to my estate plan. Why pay unavoidable future taxes at full price when the

10-pay offers me a huge discounted tax payment approach? I do love a bargain!

WHY HIGH CASH VALUE LIFE INSURANCE?

Summary and Comparison of U.S. Bank Tier 1 Capital, Fixed Assets, Life Insurance, and Pension Assets as of September 30, 2013 in $$/Billions

Bank	Tier 1 Capital	Bank Premises Fixed Assets	Life Insurance Annuity Values	Defined Benefit Pension
Wells Fargo	$116.5	$7.59	$18.2	$9.2
JPMorgan Chase	$137.5	$11.1	$10.4	$14.0
Bank of America	$146.2	$9.2	$20.3	$17.7**
PNC Bank	$28.5	$4.6	$7.4	$4.2
Bank of NY Mellon	$15.7	$1.3	$3.7	$4.6

Source: Company reports, IRS 5500s

*FDIC as of December 31, 2013, defined benefits as of 9/30/2013
**Bank of America froze its defined-benefit pension as of February 2012

Fig. 31

Let's take a closer look at this. Why is it that Wells Fargo has $18.2 billion of life insurance and annuity cash values in its tier 1 capital? Tier 1 capital is the most secure asset held by the bank in the eyes of the regulators who monitor their financial stability. So, Wells Fargo has more life insurance and annuity values on their balance sheet than they have money in their defined benefit pension plan to pay out for their own employee's future retirement benefits. They've got more of these insurance-based values on their books for their highly compensated executives than they have invested in physical bank buildings.

As of 2010, JP Morgan had $10 billion. Bank of America, who owns Merrill Lynch, had $20.3 billion. PNC Bank had $7.4 billion. And Mellon had $3.7 billion. These are huge amounts of money that these American banks have deposited into high cash value insurance-based products.[20]

---

20   Berry James Dyke, Guaranteed Income: A Risk-Free Guide to Retirement (Castle Asset Management, 2015).

BANKERS RETIRE "INCOME RICH" FROM THEIR SERPs...

Fig. 32

Let's take a look at an individual example. Bank of America's CEO Ken Lewis is guaranteed to get $3.486 million a year as an annual retirement benefit beginning at age sixty. How do you think Bank of America plans on fulfilling the promise of those benefits? Well, they're going to use what Bank of America refers to in their annual statement as a SERP. That stands for Supplemental Executive Retirement Plan.

The SERP is not the company 401(k) or a defined benefit pension plan. It's a special plan for their most senior executives. Think of it as a specially designed insurance contract.

AND THEIR BANK SERP ASSETS ARE SUBSTANTIAL

Table of Contents

Pension Benefits. The following table provides information regarding the actuarial present value of each named executive officer's accumulated benefits under the pension plans in which the named executive officer participates. For this purpose, in accordance with SEC rules, the present value was determined using the same assumptions applicable for valuing pension benefits for purposes of our financial statements. See Note 17 to the Notes of Consolidated Financial Statements for the 2009 fiscal year included in our Form 10-K filed on February 26, 2010.

Name (1)	Plan Name	Number of Years Credited Service (#) (2)	Present Value of Accumulated Benefit ($)	Payments During Last Fiscal Year ($)
Kenneth D. Lewis	Bank of America Pension Plan	40.33	678,133	0
	Pension Restoration Plan	40.33	3,265,028	0
	Bank of America SERP (frozen)	15.00	53,485,337	0
Joe L. Price	Bank of America Pension Plan	17.00	151,110	0
	Pension Restoration Plan	17.00	320,360	0
Gregory	Bank of America SERP (frozen) 15.00 53,485,337			0
	Bank of America SERP (frozen)	15.00	7,756,379	0
	Boatmen's SERP (frozen)	n/a	509,624	0
Brian T. Moynihan	Legacy Fleet Pension Plan	16.75	160,276	0
	RIAP	16.75	124,393	0
	Fleet SERP (frozen)	12.75	5,266,270	0

(1) Mr. Montag does not participate in any tax-qualified pension plans or restoration or supplemental retirement plans.

(2) The named executive officers' years of credited service under the Bank of America SERP and the Fleet SERP differ from their years of credited service under the other pension plans and from their actual service with us because the Bank of America SERP and the Fleet SERP are frozen plans. The Bank of America SERP was frozen effective December 31, 2002, and the named executive officers' years of credited service under the Bank of America SERP only reflect service through the date of the freeze. Similarly, Mr. Moynihan agreed to a freeze of his participation in the Fleet SERP effective December 31, 2005, and his years of credited service under the Fleet SERP therefore reflect his service only through the date of the freeze. In addition, the Bank of America SERP did not take into account more than 15 years of service in its benefit formula before it was frozen, and that limit is also reflected in the table. Annuity benefits under the Boatmen's SERP were expressed as an actuarially equivalent lump sum value as of the date the Boatmen's SERP was frozen and, therefore, service is not relevant to the determination of the Boatmen's SERP benefit.

Fig. 33

On that corporate annual report, they show $53.4 million in Ken's SERP. What is that really? It's some form of a high cash value life insurance policy. That's what they are using to ensure that they're able to make good on Ken Lewis's annual $3.4 million special pension. And in figure 33, we can see Bank of America has $53,485,337 of cash value in a policy to ensure their executive gets his payout. Let's think about that for a second.

Bank of America owns Merrill Lynch

Kenneth D. Lewis is the *Big Boss*

He is guaranteed $3,486,425 from BOA @ age 60

They have $53,485,337 in cash
value to meet that obligation

****6.5% Withdrawal Rate****

Bull photo courtesy Flickr user htmvalerio, used under
Creative Commons Attribution-NoDerivs 2.0 Generic (CC BY-ND 2.0)

Fig. 34

The big boss of Merrill Lynch, who would love to manage your retirement money in a managed retirement account, was guaranteed $3.486 million a year from a $53.485 million cash value life insurance policy. That's a pretty amazing withdrawal rate, right about 6.5 percent.[21] That's more than double what Morningstar told us we could safely withdraw each year, around the same time Bank of America reported this benefit in their annual report. That's a big distribution number and it's not altruistic because the policy's death benefit proceeds are going back to the company after Mr. Lewis dies. This will reimburse the cost the company incurred on this special

---

21 "Notice of 2004 Annual Meeting of Shareholders," Bank of America Corporation, https://www. sec.gov/Archives/edgar/data/70858/000119312504068314/ddef14a.htm.

type of retirement plan for their CEO. Assuming, of course, that Bank of America is adhering to the very strict guidelines that are enforced on corporate-owned life insurance policies, which I'm sure they are. I can tell you their investment representatives aren't protesting this plan. Their approach to management has to do with them using **your** money as an annuity payment to **them—interesting!**

Name	Company	Amount	Plan
Ken Lewis	Bank of America	$53 Mil	SERP
Randall Stephenson	AT&T	$41 Mil	SERP
James McNering	Boeing	$34 Mil	SERP
Muhtar Kent	Coca-Cola	$39 Mil	SERP
Brian Roberts	Comcast	$232 Mil	Split Dollar
Rex Tillerson	Exxon	$43 Mil	Add Pay Plan
Jeffrey Immelt	GE	$52 Mil	SERP
Samuel Palmisano	IBM	$28,894,991 $863,442	NQ Def Comp Qualified Plan
Marilyn Hewson	Lockheed Martin	$36 Mil	SERP

Source: Dyke, B. (n.d.). Guaranteed Income: A Risk-Free Guide to Retirement.

Fig. 35

Smart people create "SMART plans" for themselves—big company CEOs like Ken Lewis at Bank of America, with his $53 million in his supplemental executive retirement plan (SERP); Stephenson at AT&T with $41 million; Boeing's CEO McNerney with $34 million; Kent at Coca-Cola with $39 million; Roberts at Comcast with $232 million in what's called a split-dollar arrangement, yet another type of insurance-based plan; Exxon's Tillerson (our former secretary of state) with $43 million; GE's CEO with $52 million; and Palmisano over at IBM with $28.8 million in his nonqualified deferred compensation plan, which is also likely insurance based. Palmisano is the only one from Barry Dyke's research who had a 401(k) plan. The rest of them didn't.[22]

---

22   Barry James Dyke, *Guaranteed Income: A Risk-Free Guide to Retirement* (Castle Asset Management, 2015).

LOCKHEED MARTIN TO PAY $62 MILLION TO SETTLE 401K LAWSUIT

Source: http://fortune.com/2015/02/20/lockheed-martin-to-pay-62-million-to-settle-401k-lawsuit/

Fig. 36

Marilyn Hewson, the CEO down at Lockheed Martin, had $36 million in her supplemental executive retirement plan at a time when 108,000 of her employees were suing her and their pension board for the mismanagement of their 401(k).

It is interesting that today, advisors are telling people more and more to put the oxygen mask on themselves, like when you're on an airplane. Advisors are telling their clients to make sure they get all the income they need, don't worry about beneficiaries, don't worry about kids and grandkids. I have a real objection to that because I know these "kids" aren't going to get defined benefit pension plans with income guaranteed monthly in retirement. They have 401(k)s. There are no guarantees in a 401(k).

These "kids"—your loved ones, heirs, and beneficiaries—are probably not going to get Social Security, because Social Security is on the verge of bankruptcy sometime in the 2030s. In the 2030s, it's either going away or is going to be replaced by something far less benefits-rich. Does it mean no other system won't come along? I don't know. But it certainly won't be like the system that didn't work in the first place.

So I would anticipate a lesser system. "Kids" today have no guarantee from their employer, they have no guarantee from the government, and advisors have the audacity to make this all about you. I don't believe that is correct nor is it necessary. Especially since I know for a fact that you can dramatically increase your net after-tax retirement income while keeping your principal intact and continue building your wealth, because the wealth that you perpetuate onto the next generation can be tax-free through a SMART-designed inherited Roth-IRA, a SMART 401(k) plan, and/or a specially designed insurance contract (SDIC) with high cash value life insurance emphasis.

If you're willing to work a bit harder and think this through a little smarter, looking beyond the tax-unaware advisor's only-take-care-of-yourself approach, you can do more for yourself and your family by paying less in taxes. After all, the next generation needs help! If it's a choice between you and your kids or the IRS, it's an easy call. And unless you're married to your advisor, do not take their word as gospel! They are limited not only by their knowledge but by their compliance department, and their compliance department does not want them talking about taxes—at all!

Today, young people with student loans are strapped. They can't get ahead, they can't save early and get rich, and they're not going to have the same Social Security and defined benefits that their parents and grandparents have today. You also have people like these big CEOs, who really are taking care of themselves with future guarantees but are not focused on the folks who work hard for them. Today, employees are responsible for managing their own 401(k) plan assets and, with those assets, their future financial well-being.

MYSTERY BILLIONAIRE BUYS RECORD-BREAKING $201 MILLION LIFE INSURANCE POLICY

Source: http://www.forbes.com/sites/natalierobehmed/2014/03/14/mystery-billionaire-buys-record-breaking-201-million-life-insurance-policy/#5fb34e6f78b6

Fig. 37

Many readers may still think that life insurance isn't a good choice for a portion of their money. You may be right. In some cases, it doesn't fit the needs and situation a person has. But if that belief is rooted in the idea that life insurance isn't a productive product to own, then consider this: Why did this mystery billionaire buy a record-breaking $201 million policy? Do you think this mystery billionaire needs to die with more money? Or is there another reason this policy might be beneficial? Taxes ... maybe?

JIM HARBAUGH, U-M AGREED TO ADDITIONAL $2 MILLION ANNUAL COMPENSATION IN JUNE

Source: http://www.freep.com/story/sports/college/university-michigan/wolverines/2016/08/17/michigan-jim-harbaugh-contract/88910306/

Fig. 38

Do you like football? Then you probably know who University of Michigan head coach Jim Harbaugh is. Jim's a smart guy, right? So how does he get a significant portion of his compensation? In the form of an annual life insurance premium, a $2 million annual payment to the insurance company for a period of seven years. It's estimated that based on the $2 million annual premium ($14 million in total over seven years), after the insurer pays the expense of his plan back to the university at his death, there could be as much as $20 million left, tax-free, for his wife, his kids, and his trust. This split-dollar plan is going to support him in retirement with tax-free income, it's going to pay back the school the compensation they paid their coach, and it's going to leave his wife, his kids, and his trust with a large amount of completely tax-free wealth for their future.[23]

---

23   Mark Snyder and Steve Berkowitz, "Jim Harbaugh, U-M agreed to $2-million additional compensation in June," Detroit Free Press, August 17, 2016, http://www.freep.com/story/sports/college/

Jim will retire with a significant tax-free income.

Life insurance can be used successfully to create significant income if you have an advisor who knows how to actually design it for that purpose. In the next chapter, I reveal my SMART Kai-Zen design—and I'm confident it's a better plan than Coach Harbaugh's … just not as big.

The point is that large institutions love life insurance. That's why banks use it to offset the costs of employee benefits, yielding a higher return with a bank-owned life insurance (BOLI) policy than they would if they invested those premium dollars elsewhere. This is one reason we use life insurance to fund our SMART 401(k) Planz.

Trusts aren't just for football coaches like Jim Harbaugh. They can benefit people like you and me, as well.

There are many types of trusts, but the most basic is a revocable trust, sometimes referred to as a living trust. A revocable trust is advisable when you have after-tax accounts (not your IRAs, 401(k)s, 403(b)s, or other pretax retirement plans), and you do not want them to go through probate. In most states, a revocable trust directs your estate privately, so there is neither a public announcement nor a judge involved in making sure your estate is settled without debt. A revocable trust can also distribute money over time, if your goal is to spread distribution to your family for many years after you pass away.

university-michigan/wolverines/2016/08/17/michigan-jim-harbaugh-contract/88910306/.

Many times, we see trusts distributed this way when the grandchildren are young. As you can see, the benefits of using a revocable trust can be great. Revocable trust owners must be aware that if they become disabled, their successor trustee must follow their instructions. In essence, the trust can be revoked or changed by you, but your child who takes over in the event you are disabled does not have that same flexibility.

The biggest possible misstep with a revocable trust comes when you, as the grantor of the trust, become disabled and your adult child takes over when there is language specific to healthcare and your direction to pay for that care from your trust. In this situation, the protection of your assets from long-term care medical spend-down is lost.

Irrevocable trusts can have many strings attached. You need to know what those are before you enter into an agreement that cannot be changed without court involvement. Irrevocable trusts are great for holding life insurance outside of your taxable estate, if you have no intention of getting to your cash value in the future. Some irrevocable trust planning makes sense when certain types of real estate are involved. Experienced elder law attorneys know how to create hybrid trusts that offer some of the desirable benefits of an irrevocable trust, while offering more flexibility and fewer problematic strings attached.

You cannot wrap a trust around your IRA. Your IRA is a pretax asset, and it is directed at your death by beneficiary designations. It is critical that you keep a copy of your beneficiary designation form with your legal documents. In the event that you die and the custodian cannot find your IRA beneficiary designation, your IRA is paid to your estate and ends up becoming a probate asset that goes through the full process of probate. This cost and delay of probate can easily be avoided by maintaining a copy of your IRA beneficiary designation form. But a Roth IRA trust can be a very valuable tool to distribute your tax-free assets throughout your family with any specific instructions you'd like honored by the trustee and your heirs.

In many situations, trusts make sense, but if the trusts are not funded, the benefits are lost. All too often a person seeks out the least-expensive trust option, desiring value for their money, but ends up getting absolutely nothing. Once you have a trust, you must link it to the accounts you want so they are governed by the terms and conditions of your trust (could be revocable or irrevocable).

For instance, if you have a CD at Happy People's Bank for $100,000, and you want it to be distributed to your family through your revocable trust but the statement comes and it is your name on the account registration, then none of the benefits of the trust are realized. The CD will go through probate and the instructions you left behind at your death will be ignored.

Funding a trust is not hard. You do, however, need to make sure that all your financial institutions have a copy of the trust reflecting the trust as owner of your assets rather than you.

Finally, it's essential that you get help from a qualified attorney who can confirm that the assets you own are, in fact, properly titled to your trust. Take some time to discuss your trust-planning options, and if you decide they are right for you, make every effort to ensure they are properly titled to your assets so they ultimately go to those you love.

UNDERSTANDING WHERE AM I AT™

For just a moment, I want you to consider a $1 million IRA. Based on the report from Morningstar, an IRA owner expecting a thirty-year retirement would benefit by receiving $28,000 in annual income, before taxes. Let's assume a tax rate of 20 percent, federal and state combined. This gives us $5,600 in taxes and a net retirement income of $22,400.

Now let's say that instead of having a $1 million IRA, we implemented some SMART thinking before retirement and took money out of the IRA over time, paid tax, and with only modest growth we ended up with $750,000 of cash value in a 10-pay life insurance policy.

On the surface, this doesn't look very SMART—I mean, we have $250,000 less! That can't possibly be SMART, can it? Well, actually, it depends on your goal. Because remember, we have to climb down the retirement mountain—and if your goal is to do so while maximizing your retirement income, lifestyle, enjoyment, and the ultimate estate value for your family, then yes, it actually may be SMARTer to have less because you and everyone you love gets more!

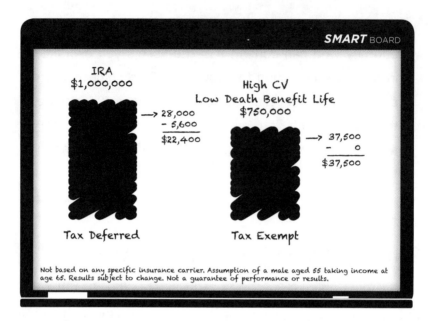

Fig. 39

As you can see from figure 39, when we assume the distribution rate is equal to other, similar plans like those we discussed before, you can see that a properly funded 10-pay policy with a top-quality insurance company, historically speaking, can sustain a distribution rate of 5 to 6.5 percent. Policies that index to the stock market may work, assuming the market returns are sufficient to capitalize the distributions. A whole life policy will work with a more conservative distribution rate. Both types of policies provide a significant death benefit through normal-aged mortality at an amount far superior to the after-tax value of having an excessive pretax IRA account, especially with the SECURE Act's new nonspousal-inherited IRA laws essentially making excessive inherited IRA values subject to income tax on an accelerated distribution to nonspousal beneficiaries.

So how can you compare an apple to an orange? After all, tax-deferred is not tax-free, and tax-free certainly isn't tax-deferred. Instead, let's consider the asset value after tax adjustments. How much money would we need to have in a tax-deferred account to net us the same after-tax income amount provided by the tax-free asset? We know from the illustrations at the current dividend rate that the insurance policy is expected to provide $37,500 per year in distributions.

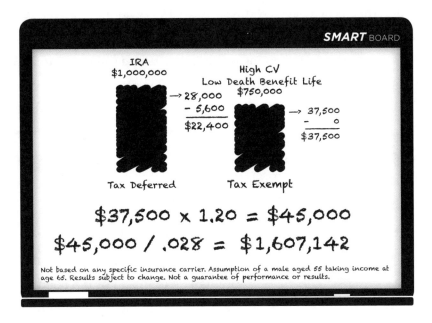

Fig. 40

That math is right: If we consider the Morningstar safe withdrawal rate of 2.8 percent, we would need more than twice as much capital in a tax-deferred account to get distributions that are, after tax, equal to those from the tax-free product. Double the accumulated capital!

As you can see, if you're planning to live off your money in retirement, the math dramatically favors tax-free distributions. And this is looking solely at a 20 percent tax rate. It's going to get even more significant, and require even more capital, to get the same net after-tax results if you only have tax-deferred accounts and tax rates go higher—which is legally scheduled to happen through a sunset provision on January 1, 2026, and may happen much sooner

Further, I expect the tax rates to continue to rise over time. And don't forget that with the tax-free 10-pay life insurance option, you also have the death benefit, which is always higher than your cash value. That benefit goes to those you love, again all tax-free. This tax-free death benefit can (and should) be used to pay the tax on a Roth conversion of remaining pretax assets, such as 401(k)s and IRA accounts after your death to enhance the value of your assets to your family. This funds the tax cost for the inheriting spouse, giving them the money to pay the income tax at a significant discount to the tax due on a Roth conversion, and enables the remaining assets to compound tax-free as a Roth IRA!

 After writing the third edition of *SMART Retirement*, we saw a dramatic expansion of the need for the Strategic Movement Around Retirement Taxation® as the SECURE Act (Setting Every Community Up for Retirement) was approved by the Senate.

Although the news around this new law has been focused on the legal delay of RMDs (required minimum distributions) until after age seventy-two, the real story is the death of the stretch IRA. With the SECURE Act, certain nonspousal beneficiaries are required to take distributions over ten years. Those exempted include qualifying beneficiaries who are:

- disabled

- chronically ill

- not more than 10 years younger than the decedent

- minor children of the original retirement account owner (only until they come of age)

This means the stretch IRA is done, and why? Because no one cares if a "rich kid" has to pay income tax on their mom's large inherited IRA.

CHAPTER 6

MY PERSONAL SMART PLAN

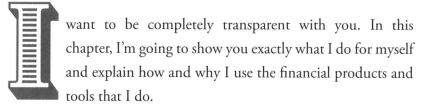

want to be completely transparent with you. In this chapter, I'm going to show you exactly what I do for myself and explain how and why I use the financial products and tools that I do.

Some of the products I use are general financial planning tools for any individual or family, whereas others are specific to me as a business owner. In both circumstances, I will let you look right into what I am doing and offer a narrative on how and why I've elected to use the planning technique I have.

First, however, I want to stress that no two people or families are the same. I'm sharing my plan with you so you can see an example of SMART in action, not as a suggestion of what you should do. A one-size-fits-all approach is never appropriate. Since each reader of this book is in a different situation— different age, different income, different asset base, different circumstances, and different goals—it means we all have different priorities and different expectations. Some of you would fund considerably less than I would or use only a few pieces of what I am sharing, while others could fund a lot more and in a much more expansive way.

My tax-suppressing/minimizing personal plan is comprised of six components:

- **A personally owned 10-pay whole life contract:** I fund this with $65,000 per year and use its growing cash values to buy big-ticket items such as cars, watches, rental real estate, and other consumer and personal investment assets. Through this policy, I'm able to borrow from myself and pay back every dollar—to the "bank" of Matt. That means every dollar I've ever put into the 10-pay continues to compound until the day I die. That compounding interest really is a miracle, just like Albert Einstein said it was!

- **A company 401(k) profit-sharing plan:** This features two components: a Roth 401(k) and a traditional, tax-deferred 401(k). I make the maximum allowable contributions into the Roth 401(k) and put my company match and any profit-sharing amount into the tax-deferred, as required by law. This is a "money-later" account invested for market-correlated growth in stocks and mutual funds.

- **A defined benefit plan:** It's here that I defer an additional $151,000 per year, with a significant proportion directly accountable to me, as a highly compensated plan participant. This is also a money-later account, but it is invested very conservatively and purposefully underfunded. More on why it's underfunded later! This plan saved me $55,870 in federal taxes on my last tax return, with a little added help from the qualified business income deduction (QBID).

- **COLI—corporate-owned life insurance:** My company pays roughly $32,000 per year to insure me as the company's key man through the COLI. This "death benefit" is one I intend to spend while I am good and alive in my retirement future, but I'll tell you more about that later in this chapter.

- **Research and development tax credits:** The R&D tax credits are one of the best-kept secrets out there. They aren't for everyone, but when you qualify, as I do, they can reduce your tax bill dollar-for-dollar up to the credit! These credits saved me over $24,688 in federal tax and my partner, Pam, over $6,100 in tax in 2019. This is not a deduction; it's the elimination of tax, something I just love the sound of! Because we have increased our efforts to innovate and better communicate via custom-built software, our 2020 federal tax credit has grown to $41,249. Again, tax credits are dollar-for-dollar tax eliminators, not a tax deduction. A $1 credit eliminates $1 of tax liability.

- **A SMART Kai-Zen plan:** I fund this with $40,000 per year specifically to access tax-free income in retirement and to add to my final estate value tax-free. This unique plan allows me to leverage other people's money and fund a balance-sheet quality indexed universal life policy. With the December 2020 changes to Section 7702 of the Internal Revenue Service tax code, our elected officials just made this SMART plan simply genius. Today, so many are swayed by the pursuit of larger and larger rates of return. The real beauty of the SMART Kai-Zen design is that it takes advantage of the realities of financial mathematics, and that's simply *volume of money saved trumps the rate of return on that money.*

Before going into the specifics of each component, let's first take a look at my tax return.

TAX RETURNS: BEFORE AND AFTER

The tax return is like the X-ray into your financial health. Nothing hurts your wealth more than excessive taxation.

When I look at the comparison of my tax return before I implemented my plan and after, it's like seeing an image of a mended bone. Take a look:

Matt Zagula
2019 Actual and Performa net of Pension and Credit

The schedule below shows your Actual 2019 return results in comparison to a Proforma return that assumes that the DB and PS Plans would not have existed and the amount paid of $151,000 would have come to Matt as a year end bonus. Also, the Proforma does not include the Research Tax Credit of $24,688.

	2019 Actual	2019 Proforma	Diff
Federal			
Adjusted Gross Income	768,934.00	919,934.00	151,000.00
Standard Deduction	(24,690.00)	(24,690.00)	-
QBID	(3,508.00)	(3,508.00)	-
Taxable Income	740,736.00	891,736.00	151,000.00
Income Tax	212,212.00	268,082.00	55,870.00
Business Credits	(24,688.00)	-	24,688.00
ACA Taxes	(3,592.00)	4,897.00	1,305.00
Federal Tax Liability	191,116.00	272,979.00	81,863.00
West Virginia			
Federal Adjusted Gross Income	768,934.00	919,934.00	151,000.00
Exemptions	(6,000.00)	(6,000.00)	-
WV Taxable Income	762,934.00	913,934.00	151,000.00
WV Tax Liability	48,466.00	58,281.00	9,815.00
Total 2019 Tax Liability	**239,582.00**	**331,260.00**	**91,678.00**

As you can see, the combination of my defined benefit plan and the R&D tax credit resulted in $91,678 of tax savings. I find it interesting that I contribute $26,000 to my Roth 401(k) and $65,000 to my 10-pay to fund my personal spending, for a total after-tax contribution of $91,000. When you look at it from this perspective, my SMART business planning (the Strategic Movement Around Rising Taxation®), the $91,678 tax savings from the defined benefit funding, and use of tax credits fully funds my after-tax Roth 401(k) contribution *and* my after-tax 10-pay contributions for my personal SMART plan, ensuring I can spend now without bank loans and that I secure a tax-free income in the future. My goal for 2020 and beyond is to find additional SMART business tax savings to cover my SMART Kai-Zen contribution of $40,000 with tax savings from my business.

Before I show you the numbers behind my 10-pay policy, I want to talk for a moment about spending. Not having a plan to spend is not smart. And yet, none of the major financial designations for financial professionals really highlights a spending plan as a key cornerstone to an overall financial plan.

If there is one thing I know to be true, it's that we (me, you, all of us) like to buy things. I have friends who spend thousands on memorabilia—they love it. I like a very specific watch—Panerai. My kid loves Jordan basketball shoes, some of which cost a lot more than my prized watches. Like us, you are very likely into something that you feel is worth spending your hard-earned money on.

Now for the economic reality of money spent. When we spend, we lose an opportunity cost that never stops compounding with each doled-out dollar—it just keeps adding up. Miss enough opportunity in your working years, and eventually, you wake up retirement age with insufficient savings to retire.

So, a dollar spent on whatever you are into or on a bill that you owe will never earn you another penny of interest after you spend it—it's gone! Even worse, that dollar's ability to compound interest is gone.

The loss of compounding is the opportunity cost of the dollar spent. But, in many cases, what's the point of working hard and planning SMART if we aren't able to spend? No matter what, we will still be spenders because it's fun and it makes all our work and effort worth it. It's rare to find the ultratight accumulator who lives a sparse, boring life to become the richest man buried in the cemetery. I certainly relate to "accumulation with family wealth transfer" motivation. I want to help my son, Charlie, launch like a champ, but I want some things for myself along the way too—my ideal approach is a balanced approach.

So if all spending and no saving is a bad plan, but all saving and no spending is also a bad plan, what's the solution? Balancing both with money now, money later and a lifetime of compounding interest.

The best place to store money for the "money now, money later lifetime of compounding interest" is in a 10-pay (or shorter) whole life insurance policy. When you fund whole life insurance, those dollars will constantly compound for the rest of your life. Mercedes Motor Credit, Chase Bank, Bank of America, Wells Fargo, and other creditors in your wallet are all diligently paid on time to keep your credit score good so they will keep on charging you an outrageous amount of interest over your lifetime. If you treat your 10-pay as well as you do those other creditors, magically, your need for their credit will disappear, and your net worth will grow ever bigger, steadily over time.

The Debt Free 4 Life software mentioned earlier in the book was devised from a spreadsheet I worked on with an Ivy League math professor, an enrolled pension actuary with a master's degree in math, and a computer programmer who was writing complex code at thirteen years old. I wanted to be sure I was being SMART with my money, and the verdict was simply that the power of compounding interest is undeniable, if directed correctly. The concept takes time to launch, but when it starts truly rolling, it's dramatic how much it adds to your accumulation of accessible resources. Now, let's see that theory in action.

LET'S LOOK AT MY 10-PAY POLICY
What's the *worst* thing that can happen?

Dur	End of Yr Age	Year	Annualized Current Policy Premium	Annualized Premium Outlay	Guaranteed Values		Net Death Benefit
					Cash Surrender Value		
1	47	2017	65,000.01	65,000.01	0		1,476,927
2	48	2018	65,000.01	65,000.01	38,489		1,476,927
3	49	2019	65,000.01	65,000.01	101,081		1,476,927
4	50	2020	65,000.01	65,000.01	166,140		1,476,927
5	51	2021	65,000.01	65,000.01	233,694		1,476,927
6	52	2022	65,000.01	65,000.01	303,878		1,476,927
7	53	2023	65,000.01	65,000.01	376,675		1,476,927
8	54	2024	65,000.01	65,000.01	452,265		1,476,927
9	55	2025	65,000.01	65,000.01	530,704		1,476,927
10	56	2026	65,000.01	65,000.01	612,083		1,476,927
11	57	2027	0.00	0.00	631,104		1,476,927
12	58	2028	0.00	0.00	650,601		1,476,927

Company has paid dividends continuously for ninety-four straight years and has been AM Best for three continuous years.

Hypothetical insurance illustration. Does not represent a specific product or insurance carrier.

Fig. 41

Above is a look at my 10-pay policy. As you look at the premium dollars rolling into it and the cash values, low in the first couple of years then shooting up, ask yourself one vital question: What's the worst thing that can happen? This policy was issued by a company that's been highly rated by AM Best for fifty-one continuous years.

This company has also paid dividends out to policyholders for ninety-seven straight years. They paid dividends to their policyholders through the Great Depression, through the energy crisis and bad market of 1973 and 1974, through the tech bubble, and even through 2008 when everything fell apart for the Great Recession. They paid dividends through all of those periods of economic turmoil.

But just in case—*just in case*—the company provides a "worst-case scenario" to show me what my policy will be worth if they suddenly stop paying dividends. And by the way, they have the right to do that. Of course, as I said, they haven't done that a single time in ninety-four consecutive years, but we're talking about a worst-case scenario. Worse than 2008, year after year—every year.

Remember earlier when we talked about basis? If we take a look at my policy, you can see that I paid $65,000 a year into the policy for ten years. That means I've paid a total of $650,000 over ten years into my 10-pay. That's my basis. Our priority there is to make sure that basis is accounted for so it can be protected and we are ensured a return of our capital and, hopefully, added gains through accumulated dividends.

Now, granted, this worst-case guaranteed value isn't ideal, but at the end of twelve years, this company has guaranteed me that they will have a definite cash value for me of $650,601. And if I die along the way, they're obligated to pay my beneficiaries $1,476,927. If I become disabled in any year after the contract is issued, then the insurer is obligated to pay premiums for me over those remaining years until the policy is paid up, so not only am I guaranteed the return of my capital but I also enjoy peace of mind knowing that I have other benefits and protections as well.

Again, this isn't ideal, nor is it my expected outcome, but at the end of twelve years, the policy issuer has a statutory obligation to have guaranteed cash value for me of $650,601 and on top of that, they're obligated to pay:

- My beneficiaries $1,476,927 if I die

- My contributions if I become disabled

- Benefits to me if I become chronically or terminally ill

So I have some real and valuable benefits that I can absolutely count on. This is the absolute worst thing that could happen to me. Now I'm guessing if it's this bad, it's likely the stock market and global economy have been a lot less kind to the 401(k) assets of my neighbors and friends. But I know I can at least get my money back from my 10-pay over twelve years based on the guarantee, my absolute worst-case scenario.

Think about this for a moment—what kind of economic disaster would it take for this company to stop paying dividends for twelve straight years? How bad would things have to get if they didn't even stop paying dividends during the Great Depression?

But let's say things do get that bad, so bad that our worst-case scenario here comes true. While I may only have my principal in whole, what do you think is happening to my money invested in the stock and bond markets? I'd be lucky if I'm getting back a percentage of what I put in. But, no matter what, no matter how bad things get or how many market crashes we endure in the future, I know I can at least get my money back over twelve years based on that guarantee, and I have that capital to reinvest if markets get hit that hard.

I've already mentioned that I like bargains, and there are a lot of bargains available during a market downturn. So for me, diversification and liquidity win!

THE NEGATIVE SIDE OF LIFE INSURANCE

Why do people and advisors get so negative on life insurance? Well, first of all, there are a lot of different types of insurance contracts, and the best-fitting contract isn't always sold. When the wrong policy is sold in the interest of creating profit for an insurance company and the insurance agent selling it, the whole industry looks bad.

One example is when an insurance policy is sold without the buyer understanding the cost of the coverage. In my case, having a 10-pay life policy, I don't have a flexible premium. Because of that, the cost component is actuarially set at the time of purchase, which is fantastic because the cost is a known factor. But, there is still a "knock."

And the "knock" is it has a bad rate of return. Your guaranteed asset, which guarantees *at minimum* a return of your basis over a period of time, has a bad rate of return. And whenever someone throws that bad rate of return argument at me, the first thing I do is ask them:

- What's bad about having a guaranteed asset and capital you can access tax-free?

- What's bad about having something that will pay the ongoing obligation for you if you become disabled?

- What's bad about having a chronic and terminal illness rider? Especially since this so-called bad rate of return is literally only in year 1—one single year!

Let the numbers speak for themselves:

LET'S LOOK AT MY 10-PAY POLICY
Accumulation: Bad Rate of Return!

		----Current Values----			
Annualized Premium Outlay	Cumulative Premium Outlay	Total Dividend	Cumulative Dividends	Cash Surrender Value	Net Death Benefit
65,000.01	65,000	5,878	5,878	5,878	1,495,935
65,000.01	130,000	6,214	12,092	50,779	1,515,374
65,000.01	195,000	6,696	18,788	120,481	1,535,637
65,000.01	260,000	7,371	26,159	193,563	1,557,217
65,000.01	325,000	8,202	34,361	270,239	1,580,453
65,000.01	390,000	9,284	43,645	350,925	1,605,904
65,000.01	455,000	10,621	54,266	435,898	1,634,090
65,000.01	520,000	12,300	66,566	525,723	1,665,699
65,000.01	585,000	14,478	81,044	621,012	1,701,741
65,000.01	650,000	17,480	98,525	722,733	1,743,920

Hypothetical insurance illustration. Does not represent a specific product or insurance carrier.

Fig. 42

Remember how I told you rate of return was only half the story? Let's take a look at the other half. Here's what they mean by bad rate of return. On the accumulation basis, $650,000 has been paid in, which is the cumulative premium outlay, and at the end of year 10 the cash surrender value is $722,733 under the current dividend scale, which represents a compounded return of a little more than 2.33 percent, tax-free.

Ignoring the fact that my death benefit has also grown during this time, if you just do the math on my cash value, 2.33 percent is not a great rate of return, even when it's tax-free. It's likely that I could have accumulated even more using traditional retirement-planning assets, such as mutual funds or stocks. But you know what else is possible in that scenario? That I could have lost a portion of my money in those more traditional retirement-planning assets to a poorly performing stock market.

What people seem to hate about life insurance is that first year, when the cash surrender value is low (or zero) compared to the premium funded into the contract. But what no one likes to talk about (or consider the possibility of) is the fact that I could die in that first year, and then the policy would have to pay out over $1.4 million to my beneficiaries. And if I become disabled in year 1, then they have to pay $65,000 a year for nine years into my policy, on my behalf, with their money.

So, it's not that you've lost money or your money has disappeared in that first year; it simply isn't accessible to you. It's being used to secure other benefits—future benefits. Like building any good business, nothing happens in a short period of time. It takes time to accumulate, but it's incredibly beneficial for your entire life as tax-free accessible cash for major purchases and supplemental tax-free retirement income.

It can also be used as a go-to resource for chronic illness to help pay those high costs, as a pool of money for peace of mind during a terminal illness, to take cash from to pay taxes on a Roth conversion, and to dollar-cost-average back into investments if the market experiences a substantial downturn. Funds can also be used after death so your spouse can pay tax on a Roth conversion of your remaining IRAs, 401(k)s, and deferred compensation pretax assets.

Let's get back to that rate of return. I do agree that the rate of return is initially low, and I don't try to hide it. But we don't live on rate of return in retirement—we live off the withdrawal rate. And the withdrawal rate on a properly structured 10-pay contract is really impressive to me.

What you're going to see here is you can have withdrawal rates of 5 to 6 percent on a 10-pay policy, compared to the safe withdrawal rate of 2.7 percent Morningstar told us we could take from a market-based retirement plan. That makes things a little bit different, doesn't it? Please understand, these rates are reasonable to assume today in our current interest rate environment. Could they be lower? Sure, but I'd argue there is an equal—if not greater—chance that they can be higher as inflation presents itself and interest rates adjust to that inflationary environment.

ACCUMULATION PHASE

Dur	End of Yr Age	Year	Annualized Current Policy Premium	Annualized Premium Outlay	Cumulative Premium Outlay	Total Dividend	Cumulative Dividends	Cash Surrender Value	Net Death Benefit
1	47	2017	65,000.01	65,000.01	65,000	5,878	5,878	5,878	1,495,935
2	48	2018	65,000.01	65,000.01	130,000	6,214	12,092	50,779	1,515,374
3	49	2019	65,000.01	65,000.01	195,000	6,696	18,788	120,481	1,535,637
4	50	2020	65,000.01	65,000.01	260,000	7,371	26,159	193,563	1,557,217
5	51	2021	65,000.01	65,000.01	325,000	8,202	34,361	270,239	1,580,453
6	52	2022	65,000.01	65,000.01	390,000	9,284	43,645	350,925	1,605,904
7	53	2023	65,000.01	65,000.01	455,000	10,621	54,266	435,898	1,634,090
8	54	2024	65,000.01	65,000.01	520,000	12,300	66,566	525,723	1,665,699
10	**56**	**2026**	**65,000.01**	**65,000.01**	**650,000**	**17,480**	**98,525**	**722,733**	**1,743,920**
11	57	2027	0.00	0.00	650,000	15,918	114,443	761,217	1,781,166
12	58	2028	0.00	0.00	650,000	17,091	131,533	801,712	1,819,964
13	59	2029	0.00	0.00	650,000	18,339	149,873	844,475	1,860,365
14	60	2030	0.00	0.00	650,000	19,744	169,617	889,688	1,902,588
15	61	2031	0.00	0.00	650,000	21,192	190,809	937,326	1,946,598
16	62	2032	0.00	0.00	650,000	22,756	213,565	987,451	1,992,516
17	63	2033	0.00	0.00	650,000	24,419	237,983	1,040,044	2,040,422
18	64	2034	0.00	0.00	650,000	26,155	264,139	1,095,132	2,090,346
19	65	2035	0.00	0.00	650,000	27,938	292,077	1,152,837	2,142,262

Hypothetical insurance illustration. Does not represent a specific product or insurance carrier.

Fig. 43

DISTRIBUTION PHASE

Dur	End of Yr Age	Year	Annualized Premium Outlay	Cumulative Premium Outlay	Total Dividend	Cumulative Dividends	Cash Surrender Value	Net Death Benefit
						Current Values		
20	66	2036	-80,000.00	570,000	29,820	321,896	1,129,588	2,112,559
21	67	2037	-80,000.00	490,000	31,768	353,664	1,105,426	2,081,072
22	68	2038	-80,000.00	410,000	33,808	387,472	1,080,398	2,047,664
23	69	2039	-80,000.00	330,000	35,943	423,415	1,054,458	2,012,193
24	70	2040	-80,000.00	250,000	38,154	461,569	1,027,633	1,974,466
25	71	2041	-80,000.00	170,000	40,563	502,132	999,753	1,934,487
27	73	2043	-80,000.00	10,000	45,971	591,264	940,219	1,847,670
29	75	2045	-80,000.00	-150,000	52,236	692,474	874,661	1,751,560
30	76	2046	-80,000.00	-230,000	55,722	748,196	839,777	1,699,962
31	77	2047	-80,000.00	-310,000	59,464	807,660	803,499	1,645,945
32	78	2048	-80,000.00	-390,000	63,388	871,048	765,503	1,589,360
33	79	2049	-80,000.00	-470,000	67,462	938,510	725,369	1,530,007
34	80	2050	-80,000.00	-550,000	71,767	1,010,277	682,714	1,467,793
35	81	2051	-80,000.00	-630,000	76,155	1,086,432	637,192	1,402,416
36	82	2052	-80,000.00	-710,000	80,695	1,167,127	588,331	1,333,664
37	83	2053	-80,000.00	-790,000	85,351	1,252,478	536,058	1,261,259
38	84	2054	-80,000.00	-870,000	90,134	1,342,612	480,169	1,184,921
39	85	2055	-80,000.00	-950,000	95,093	1,437,705	420,239	1,104,422
40	86	2056	-80,000.00	-1,030,000	100,264	1,537,969	355,726	1,019,574

Hypothetical insurance illustration. Does not represent a specific product or insurance carrier.

Fig. 44

Take a look at how my policy is expected to perform. You are looking at $80,000 a year coming out, and my basis by the age of seventy-three being reduced to just $10,000. Now if I live long enough to see age eighty-six and I take $80,000 a year out of this policy, I will have taken $1 million more from the insurance policy than I put in.

Even better, if you look to the far right on the death benefit, the insurance company is still obligated to pay my beneficiary over $1 million, tax-free. At age seventy-three, I'll still have $10,000 left in the policy. That means I will have given them $10,000 more than they had given back to me. And, again, remember on that $80,000 I took out each year, I paid no tax, but if I died at that time, my beneficiaries would walk away with $1.847 million, tax-free.

What's the after-tax rate of return on $10,000 of basis and a $1.847 million tax-free payout to my family? Good. That's what it is—very good!

TAPPING INTO LIFE INSURANCE DIVIDENDS:
It takes time but it's *so* worth it!

At 65 → $80,000/Yr. 100% tax exempt

Exempt from: Federal tax
State tax
Local tax
Medicare premium cancellation
Provisional income for Social Security taxation

No 1099!

Fig. 45

Tapping into a properly structured whole life dividend takes time, but it's so worth it. At age sixty-six, I'm looking at $80,000 a year, 100 percent tax-free. Free from federal tax, state tax, local tax, Medicare premium cancellation equations, provisional income for Social Security taxation, and there is no 1099 tax form—something you do get from the beloved Roth!

When you begin to take income out of a limited-pay policy, the withdrawals may be structured as either surrenders to basis or loans. In the case of a 10-pay policy, like mine, often the loan rate is lower than the dividend, which means you're essentially taking a loan better than interest-free—you may even continue to make gains because your credited dividend continues to buy paid-up additions, growing your cash value and death benefit beyond the cumulative effect of the loan. When this is the case, loans outperform surrenders to basis.

The most important thing to understand is that both types of distributions are tax-free. Later, I'll show you the actual tax code regarding this and explain why this is the case. It's not a loophole— it's a perfectly logical and legal move; you're giving up something later for what you are receiving now. It's float and a tax-smart, legal move.

DOLLAR MULTIPLE RETURNS: THE FAMILY GROWTH FACTOR

@ age 73 remaining basis of $10,000
Death benefit of $1,847,670
That is **$184.76 for every $1** of basis

@ age 86 remaining basis of NEGATIVE $1,030,000
Death benefit of $1,019,547

• Took over a million **beyond** basis
• Left over a million for family

Is one "BAD YEAR" worth it for all of that?

Fig. 46

So what's the growth factor here? Let's think about it from a family perspective. We'll call it the *Family Growth Factor*, as multiple dollars of return per dollar invested. At age seventy-three, I would only have $10,000 of my own money still in this contract, with a death benefit of $1.847 million for my beneficiaries. That means I'm picking up $184.76, tax-free, for every $1 that I paid in. That's a phenomenal financial result.

At age eighty-six, it becomes difficult to calculate because I have a negative basis. I've literally put my money in, I've funneled it out during my life, I've taken $1,030,000 more out of that policy than I ever put in, and the insurance company *still* owes my beneficiaries more than a $1 million—tax-free.

In reality, during retirement I will look to my deferred compensation and Roth 401(k) for the majority of my retirement income. However, if market conditions are poor and my investments suffer losses, I'll rely heavily on my 10-pay for income so I avoid realizing losses in my market-tied accounts. This will allow my assets time to recover from paper losses. A wonderful Roth reality is that Roth IRA and Roth 401(k) accounts do NOT have required minimum distributions like Traditional IRAs and 401(k)s, which would force me to liquidate at the wrong time and lock in losses.

Gandhi once said, "It is health that is real wealth and not pieces of gold and silver." I can't help but wonder, though, if Gandhi knew about high cash value life insurance, he might have more simply said, "Health is real wealth." Even if you don't have health, however, and likely can't get approved for a life insurance policy, your spouse might. You can insure a spouse or other individual you have an insurable interest in and float their future death benefit for your retirement income in the same way Buffett invests in the float of other companies. Take a look at this excerpt from an article in *The Actuary*:

Perhaps more intriguing is the huge discount to equity plus float of Munich Re. Adding back the roughly €40 billion float in its general insurance and reinsurance operations to its equity (including equity in its large life and health businesses, which is conservatively calculated) gives a total of over €60 billion. This is about three times its market capitalisation of €22 billion. Taxation of investment returns and a deteriorating reinsurance market no doubt account for much of the gap. However, it is conceivable that the shares might be undervalued. Berkshire's significant shareholding in Munich Re, the high dividend yield and the company's continual repurchasing of its own shares might support that view.[24]

Now, dividends can change. That means the numbers I've shared throughout this chapter can be different than illustrated, but let me tell you, these numbers are estimated conservatively based on where the insurance company is today and their belief about where the economy will be in the future. In better interest rate times, these types of policies could potentially perform even better. So, you can't accurately calculate how much we get beyond basis with a properly structured high cash value policy.

Now, what are you really giving up for all of those benefits and future tax-free access? One bad year—one year without access to get all of these benefits.

THE REST OF THE PLAN

Now, let's talk about my 401(k). The 401(k) is an exceptional addition to an overall approach to retirement. I put 100 percent of

---

24   "Insurance: Float-Based Valuations," The Actuary, www.theactuary.com/archive/old-articles/part-4/insurance-3A-float-based-valuations/.

my contributions into my Roth 401(k) option. I don't believe taxes will go up for everyone. In fact, I think for 90 percent of the population, income taxes will go unchanged. For me, I believe they will go up, and wealth taxes will continue to expand, so the Roth is a tax-free option I favor.

BUT ... Roth isn't the end-all many believe it to be. It has problems too. First, there is an income tax burden to funding it. There's also a payroll tax burden to funding it. Your 401(k) contributions (even those that are pretax) are made AFTER payroll taxes. They are a payroll-deducted item, not a corporate expense. So, it takes a lot of growth to make up for the tax cost. Thus, assessing your age and making a reasonable assumption of gain and the time it takes to recapture the tax cost are aspects that should be carefully considered.

Additionally, the Roth isn't for the rich. A recent discussion with a very nice, retired lawyer made me aware that the Roth has the potential to create a "financial scotoma." A scotoma is a distortion of vision, a.k.a. a "blind spot." This nice man had over $16,000,000 in net worth. He believed he would earn a high average rate of return of around 9 percent and intended to aggressively convert his $4,000,000 in pension assets to Roth. Good idea? NO.

If you spreadsheet that idea out based on his assumptions, you'll find he becomes fabulously rich! But he underestimated one important thing: TAXES. Under current law, nearly all his massive Roth IRA would be wiped out due to estate taxes. Plus, the current climate is to tax more—more of your IRA with the SECURE Act, more of your after-tax assets by the elimination of the step-up in basis.[25] Basically, the government isn't going to continue to let people die away taxes. So, taxation of wealth needs to be built SMART.

---

25   Upon printing this version, step-up in basis elimination is not yet law, but the author and the majority of subject-matter experts expect this tax law change.

Unlike the 401(k) where I want to seek high returns as a business owner, I want 100 percent safe returns in my defined benefit plan. My cost to include employees is less than the tax on me taking the income. As mentioned, it saved me over $55,000 in taxes, and it didn't cost me $55,000 in employee contributions.

Any business owner who passes on this opportunity is making a huge mistake and quite possibly is not a good boss. That may sound harsh, but I've heard business owners say, "I don't want to give my employees another benefit." Seriously? So, my choice is to cost myself less than the tax I'd owe to give a benefit to people I care about, who help me build my business?

There is a cost to doing everything. What SMART business owners do is figure out if the cost of doing something is less than the cost of doing nothing (default to tax).

A defined benefit plan is special. It's a corporate expense, NOT a payroll deduction, and therefore avoids payroll taxes. As a business owner, I know that the tax-loaded expense of funding a 401(k) is the employee and employer payroll tax—over 15 percent NOW. New tax proposals seek to increase that significantly to the point where 401(k) funding for income earners over $400,000 would have a tax-loaded expense upwards of 25 percent!

I also purposefully UNDERfund my defined benefit plan. A good actuary is like having Tom Brady on your team because they can help you crunch the numbers and get huge tax planning advantages. Why not your CPA? Ask them, and they will tell you it's two very different jobs.

Brad Barlow, SMART Planz, LLC chief actuary and my business partner on plan administration and actuarial services, opens a future contribution gap by advising me to consider underfunding my defined benefit plan. This future gap can be filled on the sale of your business! But Brad makes sure it doesn't get too big, at which point I could underfund and hit an employees' benefit portion. Instead, if I underfund by, say, $1,000,000, then later sell my business and it has a $2,000,000 gain, I can put $1,000,000 of the sale proceeds into the defined benefit plan and cut my taxable burden in half!

Every business is different, but if you have your lifestyle bills paid and get business income or a 1099 and you haven't explored a defined benefit plan, you've missed a huge planning and sophisticated tax-management opportunity.

Now on to the company-owned life insurance (COLI). Like me, my company spends money. SMART Retirement's corporate-owned life insurance on me serves three very important purposes: First, I am the key man, and if I do die, the company would struggle to replace me. The $1,500,000 in death benefit would go a long way to stabilize short-term cash flow and be sufficient to find my replacement. This is important because our clients have placed their trust in me and SMART Retirement, and I want to be assured we can live up to our service promises by providing sufficient resources to the next-in-command.

The second benefit is the cash value, which is used today to make purchases. Why would I lease or pay interest to a bank when we need office equipment or to make other large expenditures when we can use our own capital, just like I do with my own personal 10-pay? The value of compounding interest is as important for the company I own as it is for me personally.

Third, a future acquirer would get the same benefits as described, so the policy increases my saleable value, if I ever retire. A business buying my company would want to recapture cost, and the death benefit does that for them. The cash value on purchase would also be theirs. So, when I ask for the number just a little outside their comfort zone, this becomes the added "bonus" bargaining chip to get that yes at that higher number.

Now, let's talk about the SMART Kai-Zen. With the SMART Kai-Zen, you take the maximized volume approach to building your wealth and open a host of important lifetime benefits, as well.

Consider this—you have $1.00 to save at 10 percent. Will you outearn $3.00 growing at 5 percent each? No. Plus, it's common knowledge that risk and return are proportional. To earn more, you have to accept more risk. So, a 5 percent rate likely has considerably less risk than a 10 percent rate investment. Thus, we're better off increasing the volume of money we have in the game than we are seeking higher interest gains.

Some of the design decisions for the SMART Kai-Zen came after reading a brilliant article in the American Society of Pension Professionals and Actuaries journal called "Retirement Success: A Surprising Look into Factors That Drive Positive Outcomes." The SMART Kai-Zen design uses the critical component to wealth building—other people's money. I love this plan. It's "matched" with dollars "loaned" to me. I use quotation marks because it's a weird loan. No personal guarantee, no collateral, no interest payment, no loan documents, not even my signature is required. This leveraged executive plan opens up executive C-suite level retirement to the masses. It's governed by Section 7702 of the tax code and provides me tax-free future income with the leftover death benefits going tax-free to my beneficiaries.

Finally, let's talk about the R&D tax credits. These tax credits are miraculous. A credit reduces your tax dollar-for-dollar, and this credit does so based on costs for developing the software we need to serve clients. This very smart tax law encourages us to continue to develop and innovate what we do at a significantly lower, after-tax cost. Our SMART Plans R&D tax credit expert has successfully secured tax credits for over 7,000 successful business owners who reap the annual tax-eliminating benefits of the R&D tax credit.

HOW CARRIERS MAKE HIGH CASH VALUE LIFE INSURANCE

People often ask me, "But aren't these policies based on bonds? How in the world can a 10-pay dividend be higher than the current bond yield?" I want to help you understand why this is such a unique asset for you to have in your portfolio and why so many high-net-worth folks today are utilizing high cash value life insurance as an asset for major purchases, income supplementation when their invested assets are performing poorly in the market, and for tax-free income.

It's simple. When you buy a high cash value policy, your yield is based on the insurance company's general account yield. Within that general account, they have bonds that go back as far as thirty years. Bond rates may be low now, but even just ten years ago, they were higher. Thirty years ago, they were much better—a lot better than today. So you have to consider the fact that buying into a high cash value policy means buying into a vast bond portfolio with a long history and bonds with much larger yields than today's issues have.

Essentially, you're getting a piece of a mature, diversified, and well-managed institutional portfolio that's been around for thirty years, not a thirty-millisecond bond trade. You won't want to be buying a bond if there's a bomb going off somewhere, and you don't want to be in the market if something's happening that could cause a market crash—such as a trade war, currency war, impeachment hearing, or some other political scandal.

If interest rates go up, then bond prices go down. Rarely have we ever seen a time when the stock market and the bond market are simultaneously doing well. These are new-age economic risks that old strategies can't protect against. Ironically, it's my belief that an insurance product that is older than the US tax code itself offers us a viable solution for a portion of our retirement resources.

But there are added benefits. With a properly structured insurance policy, you can make actuarial profits. These are a part of the dividends that are paid to you. Let's say someone buys a dollar's worth of nonparticipating coverage. An actuary says, "We need eighty-two cents to make good on this promise." So the CEO has eighteen cents of every premium dollar collected to work with. The CEO figures out that to pay for the buildings, keep the lights on, pay employees, and keep everything working the way that he wants, the insurance company needs twelve cents. That means he has six cents left over. Who gets paid that extra six cents? The mutual participating policyholders. The reason is mutual companies don't have stockholders, so your 10-pay policy gets credited with this excess as a dividend.

Whose policies don't get credited? The people who bought non-participating policies like term, variable life, and annuities. They don't get any of the company profit in the form of a dividend. As much as I hate to see people sabotage their own retirement success with non-participating products, I know that when they're sold through the insurers that I prefer for 10-pay, they will help increase the actuarial profits that my clients will end up with a piece of in their policies.

Plus, the conservative approach taken by actuaries usually means they've set the premium higher than needed, and with 10-pay, you also recapture that "excess premium" paid as a dividend.

Not only do the participating policyholders get a dividend on an annual basis—because again, remember—many mutual companies have paid dividends for over a hundred straight years. But these mutual insurance companies may earn even more during the years when the stock market and economy are struggling. When things go bad, people tend to flee to safety, and one of the safest places to put your money (the safest place, in my opinion) is with a highly rated mutual insurance carrier. That means more premiums being paid in, and, likely, more dividends declared.

In fact, in really bad times we may be looking at dividends that are not only being supported at current levels but potentially rising, depending on what's going on at the company and with interest rates at that time. It's a wonderful place for you to put some of your safe money. It's a great place for you to buy thirty years of bond history instead of trying to buy into the flavor of the day that can turn on you in a minute.

In some circumstances, your advisor may recommend an indexed approach. Again, a highly rated insurance carrier offers you a lot of counterparty safety. With an indexed policy, your advisor will work to manage your mortality expenses and seek accrued interest through stock market index returns. It's a different approach than using 10-pay whole life, but with an experienced practitioner, you may enhance your interest gained over time.

The key to your success (or failure) is managing the mortality expenses on the policy you own since the expense is not a fixed expense as it is with whole life and will therefore change over time.

In the interest of full disclosure, I own more conservative whole life than I do indexed policies—primarily because my need for capital to spend favors more whole life than indexed life, which is more favorable for tax-free appreciation and future tax-free income. Over time, however, I become more and more balanced in my allocation between these two distinct policies.

CHAPTER 7

IS IT YOUR TIME TO GET SMART?
I HOPE SO. HERE'S WHY.

 can offer you two simple reasons to add a SMART component to your planning immediately:

1. You really should consider taking advantage of float. You can achieve enhanced, tax-diversified results using a personal financial version of float—similar to what Warren Buffett does at the corporate level at Berkshire Hathaway. Why wouldn't you diversify with a concept that excites America's top investor?

2. You'd also be SMART to fund or convert to a tax-free source of capital that can be distributed to you to supplement your postretirement income tax-free. Now take a look at page twenty-seven from the United States General Accounting Office Report to the Chairman, Committee on Finance,

US Senate, and the Chairman Committee on Ways and Means, House of Representatives on the Tax Treatment of Life Insurance and Annuity Accrued Interest.

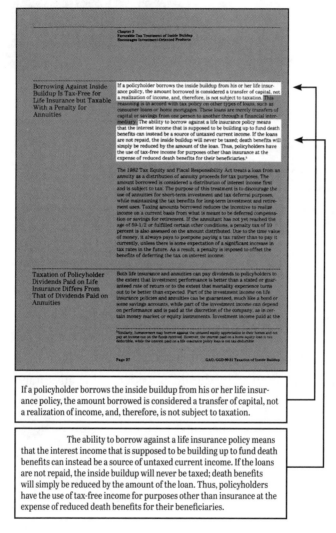

Fig. 47

You'll accomplish both of these things by implementing a SMART plan that includes a high cash value policy. What I am sharing with you is a method to create tax-free income to live off of in retirement and use to finance major lifetime purchases, taken from the float from your death benefit. Yes, I am saying you can take tax-free distributions financed off the value of your future dead self. Creepy, I know, but let's look at what the GAO says in their tax policy about the tax treatment of life insurance to see exactly how this is done.

Many advisors get excited by this sentence right here:

If a policyholder borrows the inside buildup from his or her life insurance policy, the amount borrowed is considered a transfer of capital, not a realization of income, and therefore, is not subject to tax.

But for me, it's this sentence in the GAO report that explains how you can profit from float, much like Warren Buffett does.[26] That sentence reads:

The ability to borrow against a life insurance policy means that the interest income that is supposed to be building up to fund a death benefit can instead be a source of untaxed current income.

Now it gets even more specific here:

If the loans are not repaid, the inside buildup will never be taxed; death benefits will simply reduce the amount of the loan. Thus, policyholders have the use of tax-free income for purposes other than insurance at the expense of reduced death benefits for their beneficiaries.

---

26   US General Accounting Office, "Tax Treatment of Life Insurance and Annuity Accrued Interest," www.gao.gov/assets/150/148632.pdf.

That is exactly how you benefit from float and create tax-free income for yourself in retirement and still leave a significant tax-free inheritance to your family. **But take note: This isn't a free lunch. There is an expense. Your eventual death benefit will be smaller based on your untaxed distributions. It's important to understand this isn't a tax loophole; it is a financial decision to forfeit a portion of one benefit in favor of another**.

It is incredible that more people aren't aware that with a properly constructed life policy you can, in fact, receive significant tax-advantaged income just like from a Roth IRA. But unlike a Roth IRA, you can receive income before you retire or reach age 59.5 without penalty. This income, and access to your cash value to pay for cars, college, vacation homes, and more, is a function of you choosing to float the value of your future dead self to live more financially well off today and potentially leave more generously to the people you love most when you die.

Your surviving spouse can use that death benefit to pay the inevitable taxes they'll owe on the IRA. They can even pay the taxes on a Roth conversion at a significant discount from the tax cost using the tax-free death benefit. SMART is simple; it just takes more effort on the part of the advisor who serves you. This is why I highly recommend that you work with the SMART Advisor Network member who gave you this book.

My discovery of the SMART plan was much like your own. It was all about becoming aware of the math—just as I've shown you in this book. For me, I place my trust in math over markets. The math here suggests you can live better in retirement and leave more wealth to those you love if you become more aware of methods to reduce your effective tax costs and, if it applies, your effective loss on the interest payable on the debts you owe. And that is really what SMART is all about. Pay less and get more!

TIME TO GET SMART?

After reading this, you may be wondering if this is your time to get SMART. The easy answer is that there is no wrong time to create a plan that focuses on the Strategic Movement Around Retirement Taxation®. Not only is it never too late to get started, but with the power of compounding at play, it's never too soon!

SMART isn't the traditional planning path popularized by big banks and Wall Street, who profit from the math they teach and want you to believe in. SMART is a basis-focused approach to compounding your wealth by floating the insurance company's long-term liability payable to you at your death and tapping into it as a current untaxed income at the expense of a larger death benefit later. It's not a loophole—it's common sense. The tax authority has this right: give up some future death benefit to get some advantageous income. The December 2020 tax revision to Section 7702 only further enhances the benefit of adding a plan like this to your retirement.

So why not go ahead and get started? Get SMART and get financially ahead—today. Learn how 10-pay, the Roth IRA, a SMART Kai-Zen, and Roth 401(k) are your best resources to building greater tax diversification, resulting in more net-spendable dollars for you in your retirement, greater tax-free wealth for your family, and possibly BOTH!

To learn more about SMART, contact the SMART Advisor Network member who gave you this book. **Lastly, always remember that every dollar you have either compounds for you or compounds for someone else. Make the SMART move and compound your wealth and income for yourself and your family.**

ABOUT THE SMART ADVISOR NETWORK

Members of the SMART Advisor Network are dedicated to protecting the financial well-being of the clients they serve. Since the network's inception, members have been maximizing the benefit of their collective wisdom in the financial, tax-aware planning, debt-elimination, float, and insurance areas of their practices. They meet often to review new methods of preserving clients' wealth and improving the tax-efficiency of postretirement income and eliminating any debt along the way.

Members work to preserve their clients' financial well-being with greater tax awareness, driving down effective tax costs and effective interest costs as low as possible using the SMART techniques outlined in this book.

ABOUT THE AUTHOR

Matt Zagula, founder of SMART Retirement, likens his professional journey to the mountain climb that retirees make. Matt spent years accumulating knowledge from many different perspectives with the idea that when he finally hit that pinnacle of the mountain, he would be well prepared to distribute quality advice that could be accounted for mathematically and not rely on hypothetical market illustrations. His goal was, and remains, to provide advice with confidence based on fact—not fiction.

Matt has followed a unique path, from being a very early adopter and pioneer in what is known today as income planning, to creating a distinctive practice model and level of notoriety in the industry that allowed his firm to be acquired in 2001, when Matt was just thirty-one, by a publicly traded company, National Financial Partners (NYSE Symbol: NFP). After the market crash in 2008, Matt purchased his firm back from NFP at a huge discount using his life insurance cash value to make this smart investment at the perfect time. He remains independent to this day.

Today, Matt is the cofounder of SMART Planz, LLC, a premier provider of tax-aware 401(k) plan design and SMART Retirement, the country's first mutual and fraternal company-focused marketing organization serving the members of the SMART Advisor Network. His focus is on helping preretirees and those in retirement get more—more income, more financial freedom, and more peace of mind knowing their plans are built on a solid foundation using the commonsense SMART Retirement Planning Process. Matt has spent decades continually adapting and evolving the model, and today, he is considered to be a thought leader and planning innovator for tax, estate, and retirement income advanced-plan designs.

Matt is dedicated to helping people and business owners profit from differences in the way their money is treated for tax purposes. Actuarially, he helps them realize profits by reversing the traditional use of certain insurance-based products, creating attractive returns and results for his clients, resulting in greater retirement income and real wealth. His practice has evolved into the creation of insurance-based products and serving top insurance companies in an effort to make SMART Retirement products available to Americans working toward and in retirement. These products are distributed exclusively through advisors within the SMART Advisor Network.

Although he has been retained in the past to work with advisors from insurance distribution firms with annual sales volumes of $1 to $5 billion, Matt now focuses on a very small and specialized group of advisors within the SMART Advisor Network. This narrow focus assures the public that any advisor, CPA, or law firm that is a member of the SMART Advisor Network is well trained and equipped to help their client Strategically Move Around Retirement Taxation®.

APPENDIX: CHARTS AND GRAPHS

Tax Smart 4 Life™

A SMART Roth Conversion Later™ Approach

Prepared for:

Bill and Sally

Prepared By:

Thurston Howell

Thurston@email.com

Scope of Analysis Disclaimer:

The analysis contained herein is conceptual in nature and provided to offer you a plan to pay future income taxes on your beneficiary's inherited pretax accounts. The Tax Smart 4 Life™ approach uses specific forms of life insurance to provide a death benefit for Roth Conversion at your death to effectuate a discounted tax cost based on the difference between the amount of premium paid to purchase the future death benefit compared to paying the future taxes on the inherited retirement account(s).

The report does not provide tax, legal or investment advice. The rates of return used are hypothetical and the assumptions are provided by you to illustrate future performance based on your assumptions. The life insurance projections are estimates provided by the carrier, at the time of this report, based on current economic conditions, current insurance expenses, and policy performance assumptions, which are subject to change. The assumptions used to generate this report are estimates to help you gain more tax awareness, not to endorse or recommend any specific product. You should consult your tax advisor regarding taxation, both federally and state specific.

The results of this analysis are heavily reliant on the data you provided and your beliefs about long-term reasonable rates of return and future tax policy. As time progresses, you will likely find your assumptions to be inaccurate. In addition, the insurance company illustration may also prove inaccurate over time compared to the original illustration attached hereto. This report is conceptual and is for educational purposes only.

Here is what you have entered:

Birth date:	**Jan 01, 1960**
Your expected retirement age (when retirement income will start):	66
Your life expectancy:	85
Annual CONTRIBUTION TO pretax assets (IRA, 401(k), 403(b) or pension plan) until retirement age:	$34,000.00
Annual INCOME FROM pretax assets during retirement:	$30,000.00
Current pretax account balance (IRA, 401(k), 403(b) or pension plan):	$1,480,000.00
Expected percentage annual return on their retirement account investments:	6.00%
Annual cost-of-living adjustment percentage:	2.50%
Current federal + state tax rate, taking into account extra income for life insurance premium payment:	22.00%
Expected future federal + state income tax rate on inherited IRA assets (SECURE Act provisions applied):	35.00%

SECTION 1: EXCESS PRETAX CAPITAL DEFINED AND CALCULATED

Excess Pretax Capital in this report is defined as the amount of IRA, 401(k), 403(b), SEP IRA or other deferred compensation plan where taxes have been deferred that remain in your pretax account on the date of your death after your retirement income needs are financially satisfied.

Excess Pretax Capital is estimated by starting with your current IRA balance of $1,480,000, subtracting the amount withdrawn each year, adding any projected return on investment, and repeating this for each year until your estimated life expectancy of age 85.

Estimated Account and Balance Information
Including Required Minimum Distributions (RMD)

Calendar year	Beg of year	Age	IRA balance	RMD %	Annual RMD	Annual income
2020	1	60	$1,602,800	0.00%	$0	$0
2021	2	61	$1,732,968	0.00%	$0	$0
2022	3	62	$1,870,946	0.00%	$0	$0
2023	4	63	$2,017,202	0.00%	$0	$0
2024	5	64	$2,172,235	0.00%	$0	$0
2025	6	65	$2,336,569	0.00%	$0	$0
2026	7	66	$2,446,763	0.00%	$0	$30,000
2027	8	67	$2,562,819	0.00%	$0	$30,750
2028	9	68	$2,685,069	0.00%	$0	$31,518
2029	10	69	$2,813,866	0.00%	$0	$32,306
2030	11	70	$2,949,584	0.00%	$0	$33,114
2031	12	71	$3,092,617	0.00%	$0	$33,942
2032	13	72	$3,149,997	3.91%	$128,176	$128,176
2033	14	73	$3,203,768	4.05%	$135,229	$135,229

This illustration is for educational purposes only.
Tax Smart 4 Life™ is a product of SMART Retirement Corporation.

			Estimated Account and Balance Information			
			Including Required Minimum Distributions (RMD)			
Calendar year	Beg of year	Age	IRA balance	RMD %	Annual RMD	Annual income
2034	15	74	$3,253,022	4.21%	$142,971	$142,971
2035	16	75	$3,297,517	4.37%	$150,686	$150,686
2036	17	76	$3,336,329	4.55%	$159,039	$159,039
2037	18	77	$3,369,586	4.72%	$166,923	$166,923
2038	19	78	$3,395,673	4.93%	$176,087	$176,087
2039	20	79	$3,414,763	5.13%	$184,649	$184,649
2040	21	80	$3,425,998	5.35%	$193,651	$193,651
2041	22	81	$3,428,554	5.59%	$203,004	$203,004
2042	23	82	$3,421,662	5.85%	$212,604	$212,604
2043	24	83	$3,404,267	6.14%	$222,695	$222,695
2044	25	84	$3,375,412	6.46%	$233,110	$233,110
2045	26	85	$3,336,068	6.76%	$241,868	$241,868

Based on your belief that your long-term average rate of return will be 6.00%, your current age of 60, your life-expectancy estimate of age 85, and an annual income in retirement of $30,000 starting at your retirement age of 66 and adding an annual cost of living adjustment of 2.50%, you would have:

$3,336,068

Excess Pretax Capital at age 85

$1,167,624

Taxes paid at your estimated future tax rate
of 35.00% at age 85

$2,168,444

Balance remaining after taxes paid

SECTION 2: BENEFIT OF A ROTH CONVERSION LATER™

The total net benefit, after taxes are paid, of the Roth Conversion Later™ Approach compared to staying your existing course and doing nothing different than you are is $482,740.

This is based on your assumptions of future rates of return and tax rates along with data taken from the attached specifically designed life insurance policy in Section 4.

Do Nothing Different	Roth Conversion Later™
$3,336,068	**$2,311,980**
Excess Pretax Capital at age 85	Excess Pretax Capital at age 85
$1,167,624	$809,193
Taxes paid at your estimated future tax rate of 35.00% at age 85	Taxes paid at your estimated future tax rate of 35.00% at age 85
-	**$1,148,398**
No death benefit at age 85	Death benefit at age 85
$2,168,444	**$2,651,185**
Balance remaining after taxes paid	Balance remaining after taxes paid

Plan Advantage: **$482,740**

SECTION 3: ROTH CONVERSION LATER™ DETAILS DEFINED

Under the SMART Roth Conversion Later™ plan, a specifically designed life insurance policy is incorporated into your financial plan with the sole purpose of having its tax-free death benefit pay your tax liability on your remaining Excess Pretax Capital.

This results in a lower effective tax cost because the amount of premium into your specifically designed life insurance policy is less than the amount of tax owed on your remaining Excess Pretax Capital, based on your assumption of future tax rates.

Your financial advisor has chosen the specifically designed life insurance policy with the right premium and death benefit in order to cover the projected tax liability for your remaining Excess Pretax Capital.

Roth Conversion Later™ Estimated Account and Balance Information Including Required Minimum Distributions (RMD)							
Calendar year	Beg of year	Age	IRA balance	RMD %	Annual RMD	Annual income	Insurance payment (including taxes)
2020	1	60	$1,538,697	0.00%	$0	$0	$64,102
2021	2	61	$1,600,916	0.00%	$0	$0	$64,102
2022	3	62	$1,666,869	0.00%	$0	$0	$64,102
2023	4	63	$1,736,778	0.00%	$0	$0	$64,102
2024	5	64	$1,810,882	0.00%	$0	$0	$64,102
2025	6	65	$1,889,433	0.00%	$0	$0	$64,102
2026	7	66	$1,908,696	0.00%	$0	$30,000	$64,102
2027	8	67	$1,928,365	0.00%	$0	$30,750	$64,102
2028	9	68	$1,948,446	0.00%	$0	$31,518	$64,102
2029	10	69	$1,968,944	0.00%	$0	$32,306	$64,102

* Insurance premium is $50,000; amount of $64,102 required to cover taxes.

This illustration is for educational purposes only.
Tax Smart 4 Life™ is a product of SMART Retirement Corporation.

Roth Conversion Later™
Estimated Account and Balance Information
Including Required Minimum Distributions (RMD)

Calendar year	Beg of year	Age	IRA balance	RMD %	Annual RMD	Annual income	Insurance payment (including taxes)
2030	11	70	$2,053,966	0.00%	$0	$33,114	$0
2031	12	71	$2,143,262	0.00%	$0	$33,942	$0
2032	13	72	$2,183,028	3.91%	$88,829	$88,829	$0
2033	14	73	$2,220,292	4.05%	$93,717	$93,717	$0
2034	15	74	$2,254,427	4.21%	$99,082	$99,082	$0
2035	16	75	$2,285,263	4.37%	$104,429	$104,429	$0
2036	17	76	$2,312,160	4.55%	$110,218	$110,218	$0
2037	18	77	$2,335,208	4.72%	$115,682	$115,682	$0
2038	19	78	$2,353,287	4.93%	$122,033	$122,033	$0
2039	20	79	$2,366,517	5.13%	$127,967	$127,967	$0
2040	21	80	$2,374,303	5.35%	$134,205	$134,205	$0
2041	22	81	$2,376,074	5.59%	$140,686	$140,686	$0
2042	23	82	$2,371,299	5.85%	$147,340	$147,340	$0
2043	24	83	$2,359,243	6.14%	$154,333	$154,333	$0
2044	25	84	$2,339,246	6.46%	$161,551	$161,551	$0
2045	26	85	$2,311,980	6.76%	$167,621	$167,621	$0

Based on your belief that your long-term average rate of return will be 6.00%, your current age of 60, and your life-expectancy estimate of age 85, and an annual income in retirement of $30,000 starting at your retirement age of 66 and adding an annual cost of living adjustment of 2.50%, you would have:

$2,311,980

Excess Pretax Capital at age 85

$809,193

Taxes paid at your estimated future tax rate of 35.00% at age 85

$1,148,398

Death benefit at age 85

$2,651,185

Balance remaining after taxes paid

SECTION 4: SUMMARY OF BENEFITS

**Net Benefit After Taxes Are Paid of the
Roth Conversion Later™ Approach**

$482,740

Penalty-Free Illustrated Accessible Cash Value Year 10

$495,936

**Annual Percentage of Cash Growth
Year 10 to Year 11 as Illustrated:**

$19,971	3.99%
Cash value increase year 10 to 11	on $500,000 total insurance payments

**Chronic Illness Rider
Included:**

Yes

**Terminal Illness Rider
Included:**

Yes

END OF YR AGE	YR	TOTAL ANNUALIZED PREMIUM	TOTAL ANNUAL DIVIDEND	NET ANNUALIZED OUTLAY	CUMULATIVE NET ANNUALIZED OUTLAY	CASH VALUE INCREASE	NET CASH VALUE	NET DEATH BENEFIT	NET GAIN IN POLICY UPON SURRENDER	NET GAIN IN POLICY UPON DEATH
61	1	50,000.06	0.00	50,000.06	50,000.06	0	0	747,719	-50,000	697,719
62	2	50,000.06	4,479.04	50,000.06	100,000.12	41,237	41,237	757,535	-58,763	657,535
63	3	50,000.06	4,992.90	50,000.06	150,000.18	48,027	89,264	768,153	-60,737	618,152
64	4	50,000.06	5,588.97	50,000.06	200,000.24	50,263	139,527	779,690	-60,473	579,689
65	5	50,000.06	6,187.38	50,000.06	250,000.30	52,616	192,143	792,094	-57,857	542,094
66	6	50,000.06	6,781.57	50,000.06	300,000.36	55,110	247,253	805,304	-52,747	505,304
67	7	50,000.06	7,348.12	50,000.06	350,000.42	57,749	305,003	819,217	-44,998	469,217
68	8	50,000.06	7,894.96	50,000.06	400,000.48	60,574	365,577	833,754	-34,423	433,753
69	9	50,000.06	8,422.85	50,000.06	450,000.54	63,574	429,151	848,840	-20,850	398,839
70	10	50,000.06	8,939.58	50,000.06	500,000.60	66,785	495,936	864,422	-4,065	364,421
71	11	0.00	6,512.35	0.00	500,000.60	19,971	515,907	875,473	15,907	375,472
72	12	0.00	7,397.02	0.00	500,000.60	21,098	537,006	887,700	37,005	387,700
73	13	0.00	8,322.56	0.00	500,000.60	22,233	559,238	901,111	59,238	401,110
74	14	0.00	9,283.86	0.00	500,000.60	23,377	582,616	915,702	82,615	415,702
75	15	0.00	10,304.09	0.00	500,000.60	24,562	607,177	931,510	107,177	431,510
76	16	0.00	11,322.31	0.00	500,000.60	25,733	632,910	948,478	132,909	448,477
77	17	0.00	12,381.83	0.00	500,000.60	26,988	659,898	966,615	159,898	466,614
78	18	0.00	13,436.23	0.00	500,000.60	28,254	688,153	985,864	188,152	485,863
79	19	0.00	14,501.84	0.00	500,000.60	29,556	717,709	1,006,195	217,708	506,194
80	20	0.00	15,595.88	0.00	500,000.60	30,890	748,599	1,027,603	248,598	527,603

This illustration is for educational purposes only.
Tax Smart 4 Life™ is a product of SMART Retirement Corporation.

END OF YR AGE	YR	TOTAL ANNUALIZED PREMIUM	TOTAL ANNUAL DIVIDEND	NET ANNUALIZED OUTLAY	CUMULATIVE NET ANNUALIZED OUTLAY	CASH VALUE INCREASE	NET CASH VALUE	NET DEATH BENEFIT	NET GAIN IN POLICY UPON SURRENDER	NET GAIN IN POLICY UPON DEATH
81	21	0.00	16,706.78	0.00	500,000.60	32,193	780,792	1,050,072	280,791	550,071
82	22	0.00	17,644.08	0.00	500,000.60	33,269	814,061	1,073,336	314,060	573,335
83	23	0.00	18,571.92	0.00	500,000.60	34,371	848,432	1,097,356	348,431	597,356
84	24	0.00	19,689.45	0.00	500,000.60	35,426	883,858	1,122,359	383,857	622,358
85	25	0.00	20,867.30	0.00	500,000.60	36,446	920,303	1,148,398	420,303	648,398
86	26	0.00	22,115.19	0.00	500,000.60	55,110	247,253	1,175,543	457,726	675,542
87	27	0.00	23,411.14	0.00	500,000.60	57,749	305,003	1,203,838	496,031	703,838
88	28	0.00	24,753.18	0.00	500,000.60	60,574	365,577	1,233,331	535,146	733,330
89	29	0.00	26,138.32	0.00	500,000.60	63,574	429,151	1,264,067	574,987	764,066
90	30	0.00	27,514.67	0.00	500,000.60	66,785	495,936	1,296,033	615,547	796,032
91	31	0.00	28,875.59	0.00	500,000.60	19,971	515,907	1,329,211	656,838	829,210
92	32	0.00	29,864.81	0.00	500,000.60	21,098	537,006	1,363,174	698,693	863,173
93	33	0.00	30,721.00	0.00	500,000.60	22,233	559,238	1,397,767	741,300	897,767
94	34	0.00	31,434.24	0.00	500,000.60	23,377	582,616	1,432,819	784,951	932,818
95	35	0.00	31,961.02	0.00	500,000.60	24,562	607,177	1,468,090	830,295	968,090
96	36	0.00	31,705.45	0.00	500,000.60	25,733	632,910	1,502,667	877,870	1,002,667
97	37	0.00	31,540.49	0.00	500,000.60	26,988	659,898	1,536,592	928,615	1,036,591
98	38	0.00	31,011.33	0.00	500,000.60	28,254	688,153	1,569,377	984,442	1,069,377
99	39	0.00	29,744.48	0.00	500,000.60	29,556	717,709	1,600,111	1,048,603	1,100,111
100	40	0.00	27,140.64	0.00	500,000.60	30,890	748,599	1,627,252	1,127,251	1,127,251

END OF YR AGE	YR	TOTAL ANNUALIZED PREMIUM	TOTAL ANNUAL DIVIDEND	NET ANNUALIZED OUTLAY	CUMULATIVE NET ANNUALIZED OUTLAY	CASH VALUE INCREASE	NET CASH VALUE	NET DEATH BENEFIT	NET GAIN IN POLICY UPON SURRENDER	NET GAIN IN POLICY UPON DEATH
101	41	0.00	80,559.91	0.00	500,000.60	80,560	1,707,812	1,707,812	1,207,811	1,207,811
102	42	0.00	84,821.53	0.00	500,000.60	84,822	1,792,633	1,792,633	1,292,633	1,292,633
103	43	0.00	89,308.59	0.00	500,000.60	89,309	1,881,942	1,881,942	1,381,941	1,381,941
104	44	0.00	94,033.01	0.00	500,000.60	94,033	1,975,975	1,975,975	1,475,974	1,475,974
105	45	0.00	99,007.36	0.00	500,000.60	99,007	2,074,982	2,074,982	1,574,982	1,574,982
106	46	0.00	104,244.85	0.00	500,000.60	104,245	2,179,227	2,179,227	1,679,227	1,679,227
107	47	0.00	109,759.40	0.00	500,000.60	109,759	2,288,987	2,288,987	1,788,986	1,788,986
108	48	0.00	115,565.67	0.00	500,000.60	115,566	2,404,552	2,404,552	1,904,552	1,904,552
109	49	0.00	121,679.10	0.00	500,000.60	121,679	2,526,231	2,526,231	2,026,231	2,026,231
110	50	0.00	128,115.92	0.00	500,000.60	128,116	2,654,347	2,654,347	2,154,347	2,154,347
111	51	0.00	134,893.25	0.00	500,000.60	134,893	2,789,240	2,789,240	2,289,240	2,289,240
112	52	0.00	142,029.10	0.00	500,000.60	142,029	2,931,270	2,931,270	2,431,269	2,431,269
113	53	0.00	149,542.44	0.00	500,000.60	149,542	3,080,812	3,080,812	2,580,811	2,580,811
114	54	0.00	157,453.24	0.00	500,000.60	157,453	3,238,265	3,238,265	2,738,265	2,738,265
115	55	0.00	165,782.52	0.00	500,000.60	165,783	3,404,048	3,404,048	2,904,047	2,904,047
116	56	0.00	174,552.41	0.00	500,000.60	174,552	3,578,600	3,578,600	3,078,600	3,078,600
117	57	0.00	183,786.23	0.00	500,000.60	183,786	3,762,386	3,762,386	3,262,386	3,262,386
118	58	0.00	193,508.52	0.00	500,000.60	193,509	3,955,895	3,955,895	3,455,894	3,455,894
119	59	0.00	203,745.13	0.00	500,000.60	203,745	4,159,640	4,159,640	3,659,639	3,659,639
120	60	0.00	214,523.24	0.00	500,000.60	214,523	4,374,163	4,374,163	3,874,163	3,874,163
121	61	0.00	225,871.52	0.00	500,000.60	225,872	4,600,035	4,600,035	4,100,034	4,100,034

This illustration is for educational purposes only.

Tax Smart 4 Life™ is a product of SMART Retirement Corporation.

Debt Free 4 Life™

SMART

DEBT ELIMINATION PLAN

Prepared for:

Bill and Sally

Prepared By:

Thurston Howell

Thurston@email.com

Scope of Analysis Disclaimer:

The analysis contained herein is conceptual in nature and provided to offer you an alternate plan to eliminate your current debts. The Debt Free 4 Life™ approach uses a specific type of whole life insurance policy heavily funded with paid-up additions, which are accessible via policy loans to pay off your outstanding debts.

The report does not provide tax, legal, accounting or investment advice. The rates of return are hypothetical and cannot project future performance. The whole life product representations are estimates based on current economic conditions and policy dividend rates, which are subject to change by the carrier without notice. The assumptions used to generate this report are estimates and not product specific. You should consult your tax advisor regarding taxation, both federally and state specific.

The results of this analysis are heavily reliant on the data you provide concerning your outstanding debts. As time progresses, you may take additional loans, which will significantly change the outcome. In addition, the whole life company may change their dividend rates and loan rates, which will also change the outcome of this analysis. This report is conceptual and is for educational purposes only.

SECTION 1: EFFECTIVE INTEREST COST ON YOUR NEXT PAYMENT

Debt	Balance	Interest rate	Payment	Monthly interest	Eff. int. cost
Chase (credit card)	$2,350	16.99%	$49	$33	67.9%
A+ Financial (student loan)	$23,450	6%	$678	$117	17.29%
Audi (car)	$32,600	5.5%	$789	$149	18.94%
PNC (mortgage)	$94,500	4%	$477	$315	65.93%
Totals:	$152,900	4.83%	$1,993	$614	30.80%

SECTION 2: CURRENT BALANCE DUE VS. BALANCE PLUS INTEREST DUE

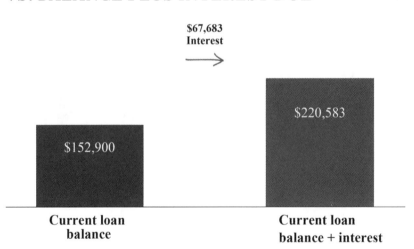

$67,683 Interest

$220,583

$152,900

Current loan balance

Current loan balance + interest

SECTION 3: DEBT FREE WHEN?

Debt	Paid with Minimum Payments	Paid with Debt Free 4 Life™	Paid with Debt Free 4 Life™
Chase (credit card)	81 months/6.75 years $1,610 interest	7 months $228 interest	$1,382
A+ Financial (student loan)	39 months/3.25 years $2,361 interest	25 months/2.08 years $2,057 interest	$304
Audi (car)	46 months/3.83 years $3,624 interest	34 months/2.83 years $3,352 interest	$272
PNC (mortgage)	324 months/27.0 years $60,087 interest	67 months/5.58 years $18,288 interest	$41,798
100% Paid Off:	Mar 2047	Oct 2025	Saved $43,757

With Debt Free 4 Life™, you will pay off your debt
257 months/21.42 years faster, saving you **$43,757!**

Your Debt Free 4 Life™ Action Plan and Timeline

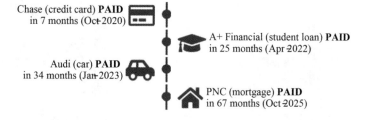

Chase (credit card) **PAID**
in 7 months (Oct 2020)

A+ Financial (student loan) **PAID**
in 25 months (Apr 2022)

Audi (car) **PAID**
in 34 months (Jan 2023)

PNC (mortgage) **PAID**
in 67 months (Oct 2025)

SECTION 4: ESTIMATED CAPITAL AFTER YOUR DEBTS ARE PAID

Debt Free 4 Life™ is a very effective method to eliminate debt. However, with the traditional debt snowball, you will always need to return to the banks, auto financiers, and credit card companies for your next purchase.

Once a dollar is spent, you don't have it to make your next purchase. With Debt Free 4 Life™, your debts get paid off, plus there is accumulated capital available to you that you then "loan" to yourself. By making yourself the only banker you will need in the future (after you pay off your current debts), you will save significant dollars otherwise lost to the interest expense of future mortgages, student loans, auto loans, credit cards and other forms of borrowed money.

The most important aspect of Debt Free 4 Life™ is to be HONEST with yourself. The key to Debt Free 4 Life™ success is that you make sure you pay back your whole life policy the dollar amount a commercial bank would have charged you. Over time, this accumulated capital will help you make future major purchases and keep you out of debt for life. Eventually, when you are in retirement, the capital you've accumulated can be used for major purchases.

Based on the illustrated values of the policy ledger attached below, which are subject to change due to varying dividend rates, interest rates and other market conditions, the Debt Free 4 Life™ advisor guiding you through the Debt Free 4 Life™ process, Thurston Howell, estimates a cash value of $83,459 by the end of policy year 8, based solely on information provided in the attached illustration.

*This estimate is for educational purposes only and likely inaccurate due to additional purchases you make, new debts you incur, by the modification of your payment schedules or changes in the dividend and/or loan rates made by the Insurance Policy Carrier over this extended period of time.

Your Debt Free 4 Life™ advisor will continue to guide you through the process and help you focus on compounding interest for yourself and not for the lending institutions lending you money at your expense. The advisor providing this information to you is an independent advisor. SMART Retirement Corporation is not responsible for the recommendations made by the independent advisor providing you this analysis.

SECTION 5: SUMMARY OF DEBT FREE 4 LIFE™ BENEFITS

Total Debt Free 4 Life™
Benefits
$127,216

Accumulated Net Cash Value
$83,459

Interest Savings
$43,757

END OF YR AGE	YR	TOTAL ANNUALIZED PREMIUM	TOTAL ANNUAL DIVIDEND	NET ANNUALIZED OUTLAY	CUMULATIVE NET ANNUALIZED OUTLAY	CASH VALUE INCREASE	NET CASH VALUE	NET DEATH BENEFIT	NET GAIN IN POLICY UPON SURRENDER	NET GAIN IN POLICY UPON DEATH
35	1	12,006.96	379.71	12,006.96	12,006.96	6,039	6,039	815,000	-5,968	802,993
36	2	12,006.96	863.82	12,006.96	24,013.92	6,714	12,753	819,058	-11,261	795,044
37	3	12,006.96	988.37	12,006.96	36,020.88	8,729	21,482	819,535	-14,539	783,515
38	4	12,006.96	1,131.02	12,006.96	48,027.84	11,231	32,712	820,073	-15,315	772,046
39	5	12,006.96	1,314.47	12,006.96	60,034.80	11,756	44,469	820,752	-15,566	760,717
40	6	12,006.96	1,592.21	12,006.96	72,041.76	12,388	56,856	821,824	-15,185	749,782
41	7	12,006.96	1,804.28	12,006.96	84,048.72	12,966	69,822	822,535	-14,227	738,486
42	8	12,006.96	2,033.04	12,006.96	96,055.68	13,637	83,459	823,481	-12,597	727,425
43	9	0.00	863.67	0.00	96,055.68	3,572	87,031	351,626	-9,025	255,571
44	10	0.00	976.07	0.00	96,055.68	3,810	90,841	355,446	-5,214	259,390
45	11	0.00	1,013.48	0.00	96,055.68	3,985	94,826	359,286	-1,229	263,230
46	12	0.00	1,062.26	0.00	96,055.68	4,174	99,000	363,182	2,944	267,127
47	13	0.00	1,108.40	0.00	96,055.68	4,370	103,370	367,119	7,314	271,063
48	14	0.00	1,148.03	0.00	96,055.68	4,566	107,936	371,066	11,880	275,010
49	15	0.00	1,195.68	0.00	96,055.68	4,784	112,719	375,044	16,664	278,988
50	16	0.00	1,240.40	0.00	96,055.68	5,002	117,722	379,038	21,666	282,982
51	17	0.00	1,300.98	0.00	96,055.68	5,232	122,953	383,091	26,898	287,036
52	18	0.00	1,358.92	0.00	96,055.68	5,462	128,415	387,189	32,359	291,133
53	19	0.00	1,417.96	0.00	96,055.68	5,696	134,111	391,326	38,056	295,271
54	20	0.00	1,489.79	0.00	96,055.68	5,943	140,054	395,534	43,999	299,478

END OF YR AGE	YR	TOTAL ANNUALIZED PREMIUM	TOTAL ANNUAL DIVIDEND	NET ANNUALIZED OUTLAY	CUMULATIVE NET ANNUALIZED OUTLAY	CASH VALUE INCREASE	NET CASH VALUE	NET DEATH BENEFIT	NET GAIN IN POLICY UPON SURRENDER	NET GAIN IN POLICY UPON DEATH
55	21	0.00	1,563.09	0.00	96,055.68	6,195	146,249	399,807	50,194	303,751
56	22	0.00	1,649.86	0.00	96,055.68	6,460	152,709	404,173	56,653	308,118
57	23	0.00	1,754.68	0.00	96,055.68	6,746	159,455	408,670	63,399	312,615
58	24	0.00	1,870.17	0.00	96,055.68	7,044	166,499	413,313	70,443	317,257
59	25	0.00	2,005.02	0.00	96,055.68	7,362	173,861	418,135	77,805	322,079
60	26	0.00	2,147.56	0.00	96,055.68	7,684	181,544	423,140	85,489	327,085
61	27	0.00	2,302.34	0.00	96,055.68	8,019	189,563	428,343	93,507	332,287
62	28	0.00	2,465.61	0.00	96,055.68	8,351	197,914	433,747	101,859	337,691
63	29	0.00	2,624.74	0.00	96,055.68	8,684	206,598	439,328	110,543	343,272
64	30	0.00	2,801.38	0.00	96,055.68	9,031	215,629	445,111	119,574	349,055
65	31	0.00	2,983.03	0.00	96,055.68	9,375	225,004	451,091	128,949	355,035
66	32	0.00	3,178.85	0.00	96,055.68	9,751	234,755	457,283	138,700	361,228
67	33	0.00	3,375.83	0.00	96,055.68	10,125	244,881	463,675	148,825	367,620
68	34	0.00	3,573.87	0.00	96,055.68	10,524	255,405	470,256	159,350	374,200
69	35	0.00	3,777.59	0.00	96,055.68	10,925	266,331	477,022	170,275	380,966
70	36	0.00	3,996.67	0.00	96,055.68	11,343	277,673	483,988	181,618	387,932
71	37	0.00	4,227.02	0.00	96,055.68	11,763	289,436	491,161	193,380	395,105
72	38	0.00	4,488.75	0.00	96,055.68	12,175	301,612	498,581	205,556	402,525
73	39	0.00	4,773.64	0.00	96,055.68	12,586	314,198	506,273	218,142	410,217
74	40	0.00	5,072.79	0.00	96,055.68	12,991	327,189	514,246	231,133	418,190

This illustration is for educational purposes only.
Debt Free 4 Life™ is a product of SMART Retirement Corporation.

END OF YR AGE	YR	TOTAL ANNUALIZED PREMIUM	TOTAL ANNUAL DIVIDEND	NET ANNUALIZED OUTLAY	CUMULATIVE NET ANNUALIZED OUTLAY	CASH VALUE INCREASE	NET CASH VALUE	NET DEATH BENEFIT	NET GAIN IN POLICY UPON SURRENDER	NET GAIN IN POLICY UPON DEATH
75	41	0.00	5,397.16	0.00	96,055.68	13,404	340,593	522,526	244,537	426,470
76	42	0.00	5,727.28	0.00	96,055.68	13,811	354,404	531,109	258,348	435,053
77	43	0.00	6,047.33	0.00	96,055.68	14,226	368,630	539,967	272,574	443,911
78	44	0.00	6,377.93	0.00	96,055.68	14,656	383,286	549,104	287,230	453,048
79	45	0.00	6,697.52	0.00	96,055.68	15,082	398,368	558,494	302,312	462,438
80	46	0.00	7,032.88	0.00	96,055.68	15,522	413,890	568,148	317,834	472,092
81	47	0.00	7,379.10	0.00	96,055.68	15,941	429,831	578,072	333,775	482,016
82	48	0.00	7,742.32	0.00	96,055.68	16,344	446,175	588,280	350,119	492,224
83	49	0.00	8,099.84	0.00	96,055.68	16,759	462,934	598,756	366,879	502,701
84	50	0.00	8,570.56	0.00	96,055.68	17,157	480,091	609,640	384,035	513,584
85	51	0.00	9,064.86	0.00	96,055.68	17,527	497,618	620,951	401,562	524,895
86	52	0.00	9,584.09	0.00	96,055.68	17,861	515,479	632,715	419,423	536,659
87	53	0.00	10,142.32	0.00	96,055.68	18,159	533,638	644,973	437,582	548,918
88	54	0.00	10,716.33	0.00	96,055.68	18,411	552,049	657,741	455,993	561,686
89	55	0.00	11,320.05	0.00	96,055.68	18,628	570,676	671,052	474,621	574,997
90	56	0.00	11,901.68	0.00	96,055.68	18,827	589,503	684,880	493,448	588,824
91	57	0.00	12,472.47	0.00	96,055.68	19,034	608,537	699,211	512,481	603,155
92	58	0.00	12,758.13	0.00	96,055.68	19,065	627,602	713,719	531,546	617,664
93	59	0.00	12,948.03	0.00	96,055.68	19,172	646,774	728,299	550,718	632,244
94	60	0.00	13,019.52	0.00	96,055.68	19,385	666,158	742,817	570,103	646,762

This illustration is for educational purposes only.
Debt Free 4 Life™ is a product of SMART Retirement Corporation.

END OF YR AGE	YR	TOTAL ANNUALIZED PREMIUM	TOTAL ANNUAL DIVIDEND	NET ANNUALIZED OUTLAY	CUMULATIVE NET ANNUALIZED OUTLAY	CASH VALUE INCREASE	NET CASH VALUE	NET DEATH BENEFIT	NET GAIN IN POLICY UPON SURRENDER	DEATH
95	61	0.00	12,933.46	0.00	96,055.68	19,871	686,030	757,090	589,974	661,035
96	62	0.00	12,625.14	0.00	96,055.68	20,809	706,839	770,859	610,783	674,803
97	63	0.00	12,195.02	0.00	96,055.68	22,047	728,886	783,976	632,830	687,920
98	64	0.00	11,480.45	0.00	96,055.68	24,142	753,027	796,113	656,972	700,057
99	65	0.00	10,291.62	0.00	96,055.68	27,750	780,778	806,747	684,722	710,691
100	66	0.00	8,253.24	0.00	96,055.68	34,222	815,000	815,000	718,945	718,945
101	67	0.00	39,676.24	0.00	96,055.68	39,676	854,676	854,676	758,621	758,621
102	68	0.00	41,616.40	0.00	96,055.68	41,616	896,293	896,293	800,237	800,237
103	69	0.00	43,651.45	0.00	96,055.68	43,651	939,944	939,944	843,889	843,889
104	70	0.00	45,786.00	0.00	96,055.68	45,786	985,730	985,730	889,675	889,675
105	71	0.00	48,024.94	0.00	96,055.68	48,025	1,033,755	1,033,755	937,700	937,700
106	72	0.00	50,373.36	0.00	96,055.68	50,373	1,084,129	1,084,129	988,073	988,073
107	73	0.00	52,836.61	0.00	96,055.68	52,837	1,136,965	1,136,965	1,040,910	1,040,910
108	74	0.00	55,420.32	0.00	96,055.68	55,420	1,192,386	1,192,386	1,096,330	1,096,330
109	75	0.00	58,130.38	0.00	96,055.68	58,130	1,250,516	1,250,516	1,154,460	1,154,460
110	76	0.00	60,972.95	0.00	96,055.68	60,973	1,311,489	1,311,489	1,215,433	1,215,433
111	77	0.00	63,954.53	0.00	96,055.68	63,955	1,375,443	1,375,443	1,279,388	1,279,388
112	78	0.00	67,081.91	0.00	96,055.68	67,082	1,442,525	1,442,525	1,346,470	1,346,470
113	79	0.00	70,362.21	0.00	96,055.68	70,362	1,512,887	1,512,887	1,416,832	1,416,832
114	80	0.00	73,802.93	0.00	96,055.68	73,803	1,586,690	1,586,690	1,490,635	1,490,635

END OF YR AGE	YR	TOTAL ANNUALIZED PREMIUM	TOTAL ANNUAL DIVIDEND	NET ANNUALIZED OUTLAY	CUMULATIVE NET ANNUALIZED OUTLAY	CASH VALUE INCREASE	NET CASH VALUE	NET DEATH BENEFIT	NET GAIN IN POLICY UPON SURRENDER	NET GAIN IN POLICY UPON DEATH
115	81	0.00	77,411.89	0.00	96,055.68	77,412	1,664,102	1,664,102	1,568,047	1,568,047
116	82	0.00	81,197.33	0.00	96,055.68	81,197	1,745,300	1,745,300	1,649,244	1,649,244
117	83	0.00	85,167.88	0.00	96,055.68	85,168	1,830,468	1,830,468	1,734,412	1,734,412
118	84	0.00	89,332.59	0.00	96,055.68	89,333	1,919,800	1,919,800	1,823,744	1,823,744
119	85	0.00	93,700.95	0.00	96,055.68	93,701	2,013,501	2,013,501	1,917,445	1,917,445
120	86	0.00	98,282.93	0.00	96,055.68	98,283	2,111,784	2,111,784	2,015,728	2,015,728
121	87	0.00	103,088.96	0.00	96,055.68	103,089	2,214,873	2,214,873	2,118,817	2,118,817

GCU: Fraternal Life Co.
-
TSR% Ratio

*Higher Risk Assets & Liability Transparency
Relative to Reported Surplus*

[From Its 2019 Statutory Sworn Annual Statement]

Thomas D. Gober, CFE

Summary of Findings

GCU is a fraternal benefit society that was organized and operates under the Commonwealth of Pennsylvania's insurance statutes. Most of the higher-risk practices that are typically the focus of this type of report are not present in GCU. Accordingly, GCU is on the low-risk end of the TSR% Ratio Comparative.

INTRODUCTION

SECTION I

Thomas D. Gober, CFE

Thomas D. Gober has been fighting fraud for over 30 years. Mr. Gober is a Certified Fraud Examiner (CFE) who has worked fraud cases of all types...from Healthcare Fraud to Federal Grant Fraud to Bank Embezzlement.

But his primary focus for 30 years has been fighting to protect insurance policyholders. His policyholder protection expertise runs the gamut of insurance operations. If an insurance company abuses its policyholders via claims delays or denials, false advertising, misrepresentation of policy benefits (failure to act in good faith) or if the insurance company falsifies its balance sheet to disguise its hazardous financial condition, Mr. Gober serves some of the most respected attorneys in the U.S. to help policyholders find justice.

SECTION II

Purpose of the TSR% Ratio

If asked by my father or dear friend if *XYZ Life* is a good company and would it be safe to entrust XYZ with his retirement funding, I would know where to look. Insurance company financial statements has been my focus for 35 years. In today's environment, I would have to dig deeper than I would in years past. To give a life insurer the green light I would have to become comfortable with at least three categories:

The *solvency by reported surplus relative to higher risk assets (as defined by the Federal Reserve) and liability transparency (or lack thereof).*

SECTION III

Trends & Findings:
Identifying Non-Traditional & Higher Risk Activities

For-Profit, Stock Company, Life Industry Challenges

The for-profit life and annuity companies face a number of challenges resulting from a combination of excessive risk-taking in certain investment categories, excessive interdependence on affiliates within their own Holding Company System, excessive levels of affiliated reinsurance and lack of regulatory transparency. Many Mutual and Fraternal companies today exhibit more traditional and fiscally respectable practices in keeping with the traditional focus on policyholder protection and their solvency to best assure the fulfill-ment of long-term promises made within their policies.

A. R-Factor: Higher Risk Investment Concentrations
Relative to Insurer Reported Surplus (KEEP)

Insurance companies report the percentages of the various asset categories they invest in as a comparison to their total investment holdings. While informative for a quick assessment of how their categories are spread across their entire portfolio, it is much more relevant and meaningful to compare the higher-risk, lower-liquidity categories to the company's reported **Surplus** of $162.7 Million. GCU's relative mix of higher-risk investments to surplus is only a fraction of surplus rather than many multiples as typically seen. Even if the entire portfolio of higher risk assets was written down, GCU would still have roughly half its surplus. While GCU does have a single investment in the common stock of a wholly-owned subsidiary, it represents only 7% of its surplus and is not being used as a conduit for transfers of policyhold-er funds up and throughout its holding company system.

GCU Investment Concentrations Analysis	Surplus	
December 31, 2019	$162,741,532	
All RMBS & Other Structured	$ 3,011,606	
Hybrids/ETF by SVO	$ 36,708,235	
Total:	$ 39,719,841	24%
Affiliated Common Stock	$ 11,361,720	7%
SCH. BA - Other - No Affiliated	$ 20,776,069	13%
	$ 71,857,630	44%

Below, note that the "ACL Required" is the absolute minimum GCU must maintain or regulators must take control of the company. At 12/31/2019 the minimum was $25 Million. In simple terms, given GCU's Surplus of $162.7 Million, there is a buffer of $138 Million. So, even if 100% of all the higher-risk & affiliated paper was written off, GCU still has nearly half its surplus left remaining viable without regulatory action.

$$\text{Reported Surplus} = \$162,741,532$$

$$\text{ACL Required} = \$\ 25,011,806$$

$$\text{Buffer Before Receivership} = \$137,729,726$$

$$\text{Total of Higher Risk/Affiliated} = \$\ 71,857,630$$

[Even if 100% of all higher risk assets failed,
GCU is solvent with roughly half of surplus left]

B. T-Factor: Transparency & Excessive Reliance on Affiliated & Wholly Owned Reinsurance (KEEP)

[NOTE: GCU does not cede any reinsurance to *Affiliates* and has NO *Captives*.]

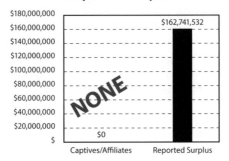

**Reinsurance Ceded to Captives/Affiliates
Compared with Surplus**

US GOVERNMENT DEBT TO GDP

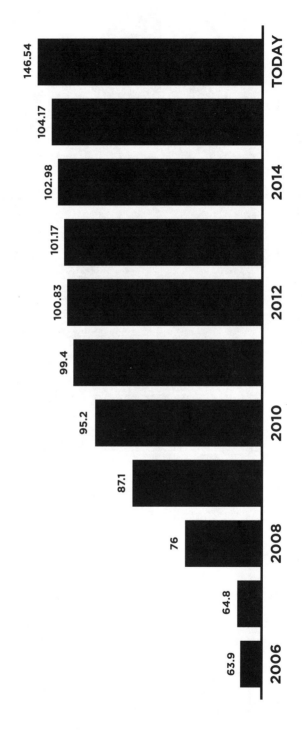

146.54	104.17	102.98	101.17	100.83	99.4	95.2	87.1	76	64.8	63.9

TODAY · 2014 · 2012 · 2010 · 2008 · 2006

WWW.TRADINGECONOMICS.COM/UNITED-STATES/GOVERNMENT-DEBT-TO-GDP

183

A TAX POLICY SET BY PERSONAL EXPERIENCE

US FEDERAL MARGINAL TOP AND BOTTOM TAX RATES - 1913-2015

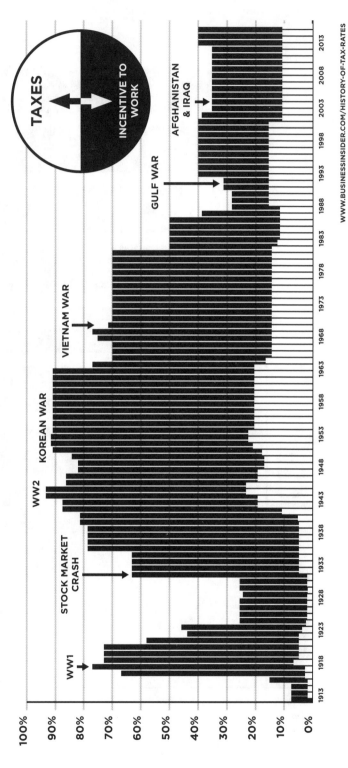

TAXES

INCENTIVE TO WORK

WW1

STOCK MARKET CRASH

WW2

KOREAN WAR

VIETNAM WAR

GULF WAR

AFGHANISTAN & IRAQ

WWW.BUSINESSINSIDER.COM/HISTORY-OF-TAX-RATES

REQUIRED MINIMUM DISTRIBUTION Table effective until 2021

Table III (Uniform Lifetime)

Age	Distribution Period	Age	Distribution Period	Age	Distribution Period	Age	Distribution Period
72	25.6	84	15.5	96	8.1	108	3.7
73	24.7	85	14.8	97	7.6	109	3.4
74	23.8	86	14.1	98	7.1	110	3.1
75	22.9	87	13.4	99	6.7	111	2.9
76	22.0	88	12.7	100	6.3	112	2.6
77	21.2	89	12.0	101	5.9	113	2.4
78	20.3	90	11.4	102	5.5	114	2.1
79	19.5	91	10.8	103	5.2	115 and over	1.9
80	18.7	92	10.2	104	4.9		
81	17.9	93	9.6	105	4.5		

Once you determine a separate required minimum distribution from each of your traditional IRAs, you can total these minimum amounts and take them from any one or more of your traditional IRAs.

REQUIRED MINIMUM DISTRIBUTION New 2021 table

Age	Distribution Period	Age	Distribution Period	Age	Distribution Period	Age	Distribution Period	Age	Distribution Period
72	27.3	84	16.8	96	8.3	108	3.9	120 +	2
73	26.4	85	16	97	7.8	109	3.7		
74	25.5	86	15.2	98	7.3	110	3.5		
75	24.6	87	14.4	99	6.8	111	3.4		
76	23.7	88	13.6	100	6.4	112	3.2		
77	22.8	89	12.9	101	5.9	113	3.1		
78	21.9	90	12.1	102	5.6	114	3		
79	21	91	11.4	103	5.2	115	2.9		
80	20.2	92	10.8	104	4.9	116	2.8		
81	19.3	93	10.1	105	4.6	117	2.7		

$1,000,000 @ 2.7% = $27,000 before taxes!!

REMEMBER MORNINGSTAR

Reitrement Period (Years)

20% Equity Allocation

Probability of Success (%)	15	20	25	30	35	40
99	5.0	3.6	2.8	2.2	1.9	1.6
95	5.4	4.0	3.1	2.6	2.2	1.9
90	5.7	4.2	3.3	2.7	2.3	2.1
80	6.0	4.4	3.5	3.0	2.6	2.3
50	6.6	5.0	4.1	3.4	3.0	2.7

40% Equity Allocation

Probability of Success (%)	15	20	25	30	35	40
99	4.6	3.3	2.5	2.1	1.8	1.6
95	5.2	3.9	3.1	2.6	2.2	2.0
90	5.6	4.2	3.4	2.8	2.5	2.2
80	6.1	4.6	3.7	3.2	2.8	2.5
50	7.0	5.5	4.5	3.9	3.5	3.2

60% Equity Allocation

Probability of Success (%)	15	20	25	30	35	40
99	3.9	2.8	2.2	1.9	1.5	1.3
95	4.9	3.6	2.8	2.4	2.0	1.8
90	5.4	4.0	3.2	2.7	2.4	2.2
80	6.1	4.6	3.8	3.2	2.9	2.6
50	7.4	5.9	4.9	4.3	3.9	3.6

80% Equity Allocation

Probability of Success (%)	15	20	25	30	35	40
99	3.4	2.3	1.8	1.4	1.2	1.1
95	4.4	3.2	2.6	2.1	1.8	1.6
90	5.1	3.8	3.0	2.6	2.2	2.0
80	5.8	4.6	3.7	3.2	2.8	2.6
50	7.8	6.2	5.3	4.6	4.2	3.9

These are the safe withdrawl rates.

Is this what being a millionaire in America has become?

SAVE EARLY, GET RICH

Comparing savings growth

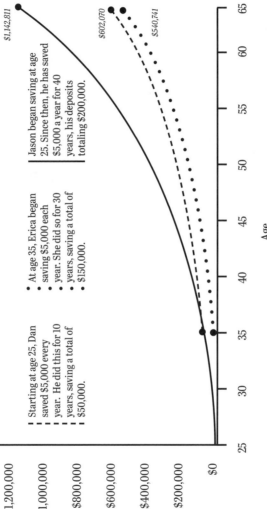

Saving Fundamentals
Saving early means gaining the ongoing benefit of compounding, which significantly increases your overall return.

Starting at age 25, Dan saved $5,000 every year. He did this for 10 years, saving a total of $50,000.

At age 35, Erica began saving $5,000 each year. She did so for 30 years, saving a total of $150,000.

Jason began saving at age 25. Since then, he has saved $5,000 a year for 40 years, his deposits totaling $200,000.

Saving

Age

$1,142,811

$602,070

$540,741

THE DANGERS OF AN AVERAGE RATE OF RETURN

Beginning retirement asset value = $1,000,000   10% of beginning value = ($100,000)
Number of years = 30   Average return = 14.84%

Constant Returns

Retirement Year	Annual Return	Annual Income	Account Value
1	14.84%	-$100,000	$1,033,290
2	14.84%	-$100,000	$1,072,100
3	14.84%	-$100,000	$1,116,360
4	14.84%	-$100,000	$1,167,188
5	14.84%	-$100,000	$1,225,558
6	14.84%	-$100,000	$1,292,591
7	14.84%	-$100,000	$1,369,572
8	14.84%	-$100,000	$1,457,976
9	14.84%	-$100,000	$1,559,500
10	14.84%	-$100,000	$1,676,090
11	14.84%	-$100,000	$1,809,982
12	14.84%	-$100,000	$1,963,743
13	14.84%	-$100,000	$2,140,322
14	14.84%	-$100,000	$2,343,106
15	14.84%	-$100,000	$2,575,983
20	14.84%	-$100,000	$4,373,434
25	14.84%	-$100,000	$7,963,668
30	14.84%	-$100,000	$15,134,818

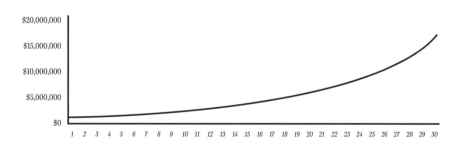

CONSTANT VS. FLUCTUATING RETURNS

Range of years   =   1970-1999   *Average* return   =   14.84%

History of the S&P 500

Year	Annual Return	Year	Annual Return
1970	3.99%	1985	31.65%
1971	14.33%	1986	18.60%
1972	18.94%	1987	5.17%
1973	-14.79%	1988	16.61%
1974	-26.54%	1989	31.69%
1975	37.25%	1990	-3.10%
1976	23.67%	1991	30.47%
1977	-7.39%	1992	7.62%
1978	6.44%	1993	10.08%
1979	18.35%	1994	1.32%
1980	32.27%	1995	37.58%
1981	-5.05%	1996	22.96%
1982	21.48%	1997	33.36%
1983	22.50%	1998	28.58%
1984	6.15%	1999	21.04%

THE REAL RISK: SEQUENCE OF RETURNS

Beginning retirement asset value	=	$1,000,000	10% of beginning value	=	($100,000)
Number of years	=	30	Average return	=	14.84%

Fluctuating Returns

Year	Annual Return	Annual Income	Account Value
1	3.99%	-$100,000	$935,910
2	14.33%	-$100,000	$955,696
3	18.94%	-$100,000	$1,017,765
4	-14.79%	-$100,000	$782,027
5	-26.54%	-$100,000	$501,017
6	37.25%	-$100,000	$550,396
7	23.67%	-$100,000	$557,005
8	-7.39%	-$100,000	$423,232
9	6.44%	-$100,000	$344,048
10	18.35%	-$100,000	$288,831
11	32.27%	-$100,000	$249,767
12	-5.05%	-$100,000	$142,204
13	21.48%	-$100,000	$51,269
14	22.50%	-$51,269	$0
15	6.15%	$0	$0

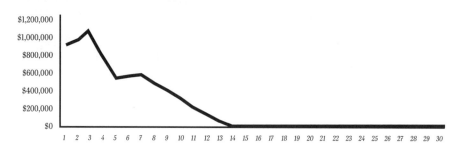

THE BENEFICIAL IMPACT OF TAX ARBITRAGE

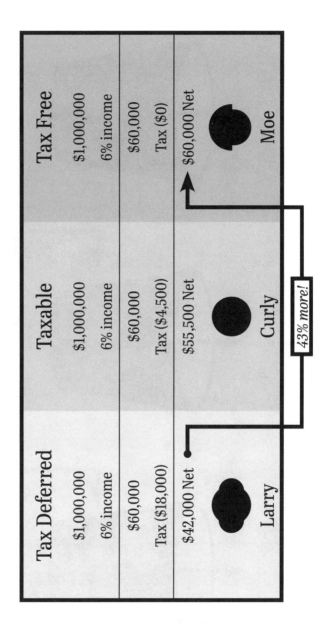

Tax Deferred	Taxable	Tax Free
$1,000,000	$1,000,000	$1,000,000
6% income	6% income	6% income
$60,000	$60,000	$60,000
Tax ($18,000)	Tax ($4,500)	Tax ($0)
$42,000 Net	$55,500 Net	$60,000 Net
Larry	Curly	Moe

43% more!

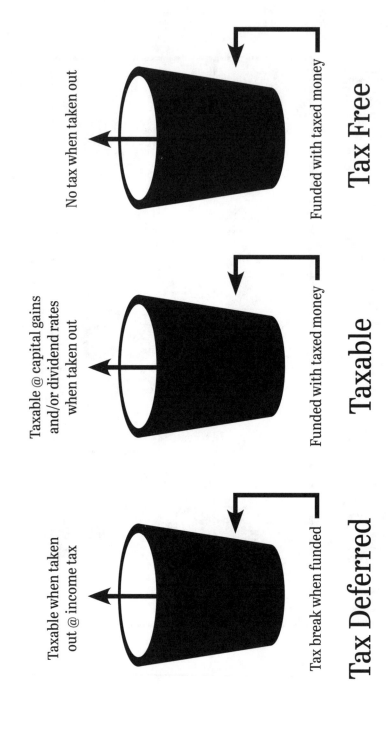

PROBLEM WITH 401K + IRAS: PROVISIONAL INCOME!

Provisional income example – Bill & Sally

50% of SS benefit $30,000 x ½   = $15,000

Annual distribution from IRA   = $55,000

Provisional income for SS tax purposes: $70,000

At $70,000 prov. income, 85% of SS taxed

85% x 30,000 = $25,500 @ 12% tax   =   **$3,060 Tax on SS!**

Total taxable income   =   **$55,400**

[$55,000 IRA + $25,500 SS – deductions ($24,800)]

Tax on $55,400 taxable income   =   **$3,339**

Total **tax** due on actual income of **$85,000**   =   **$6,253**

*For 2020, couple under 65

193

FIXING BILL AND SALLY

Move some money away from IRA to tax-exempt assets

50% of SS benefit **$30,000 x ½**	=	**$15,000**
Annual distribution from IRA	=	**$20,000**
Tax-free income	=	**$35,000**
Provisional income for SS tax purposes:		**$35,000**
Provisional income	=	**$35,000**
$1,500 SS taxable + $20,000 IRA income	=	**$21,500**
– $24,800 standard deduction		
Total tax due on $70,000 income	=	**$0**

WHY HIGH CASH VALUE LIFE INSURANCE?

Summary and Comparison of U.S. Bank Tier 1 Capital, Fixed Assets, Life Insurance, and Pension Assets as of September 30, 2013 in $$/Billions

Bank	Tier 1 Capital	Bank Premises Fixed Assets	Life Insurance Annuity Values	Defined Benefit Pension
Wells Fargo	$116.5	$7.59	$18.2	$9.2
JPMorgan Chase	$137.5	$11.1	$10.4	$14.0
Bank of America	$146.2	$9.2	$20.3	$17.7**
PNC Bank	$28.5	$4.6	$7.4	$4.2
Bank of NY Mellon	$15.7	$1.3	$3.7	$4.6

Source: Company reports, IRS 5500s

*FDIC as of December 31, 2013, defined benefits as of 9/30/2013
**Bank of America froze its defined-benefit pension as of February 2012

Name	Company	Amount	Plan
Ken Lewis	Bank of America	$53 Mil	SERP
Randall Stephenson	AT&T	$41 Mil	SERP
James McNering	Boeing	$34 Mil	SERP
Muhtar Kent	Coca-Cola	$39 Mil	SERP
Brian Roberts	Comcast	$232 Mil	Split Dollar
Rex Tillerson	Exxon	$43 Mil	Add Pay Plan
Jeffrey Immelt	GE	$52 Mil	SERP
Samuel Palmisano	IBM	$28,894,991 $863,442	NQ Def Comp Qualified Plan
Marilyn Hewson	Lockheed Martin	$36 Mil	SERP

Source: Dyke, B. (n.d.). Guaranteed Income: A Risk-Free Guide to Retirement.

LET'S LOOK AT MY 10-PAY POLICY

What's the *worst* thing that can happen?

Dur	End of Yr Age	Year	Annualized Current Policy Premium	Annualized Premium Outlay	Guaranteed Values		Net Death Benefit
					Cash Surrender Value		
1	47	2017	65,000.01	65,000.01	0		1,476,927
2	48	2018	65,000.01	65,000.01	38,489		1,476,927
3	49	2019	65,000.01	65,000.01	101,081		1,476,927
4	50	2020	65,000.01	65,000.01	166,140		1,476,927
5	51	2021	65,000.01	65,000.01	233,694		1,476,927
6	52	2022	65,000.01	65,000.01	303,878		1,476,927
7	53	2023	65,000.01	65,000.01	376,675		1,476,927
8	54	2024	65,000.01	65,000.01	452,265		1,476,927
9	55	2025	65,000.01	65,000.01	530,704		1,476,927
10	56	2026	65,000.01	65,000.01	612,083		1,476,927
11	57	2027	0.00	0.00	621,191		1,476,927
12	58	2028	0.00	0.00	650,601		1,476,927

Hypothetical insurance illustration. Does not represent a specific product or insurance carrier.

LET'S LOOK AT MY 10-PAY POLICY

Accumulation: Bad Rate of Return!

Annualized Premium Outlay	Cumulative Premium Outlay	---Current Values---			Net Death Benefit
		Total Dividend	Cumulative Dividends	Cash Surrender Value	
65,000.01	65,000	5,878	5,878	5,878	1,495,935
65,000.01	130,000	6,214	12,092	50,779	1,515,374
65,000.01	195,000	6,696	18,788	120,481	1,535,637
65,000.01	260,000	7,371	26,159	193,563	1,557,217
65,000.01	325,000	8,202	34,361	270,239	1,580,453
65,000.01	390,000	9,284	43,645	350,925	1,605,904
65,000.01	455,000	10,621	54,266	435,898	1,634,090
65,000.01	520,000	12,300	66,566	525,723	1,665,699
65,000.01	585,000	14,478	81,044	621,012	1,701,741
65,000.01	650,000	17,480	98,525	722,733	1,743,920

Hypothetical insurance illustration. Does not represent a specific product or insurance carrier.

ACCUMULATION PHASE

End of Yr Dur	Age	Year	Annualized Current Policy Premium	Annualized Premium Outlay	Cumulative Premium Outlay	Current Values			
						Total Dividend	Cumulative Dividends	Cash Surrender Value	Net Death Benefit
1	47	2017	65,000.01	65,000.01	65,000	5,878	5,878	5,878	1,495,935
2	48	2018	65,000.01	65,000.01	130,000	6,214	12,092	50,779	1,515,374
3	49	2019	65,000.01	65,000.01	195,000	6,696	18,788	120,481	1,535,637
4	50	2020	65,000.01	65,000.01	260,000	7,371	26,159	193,563	1,557,217
5	51	2021	65,000.01	65,000.01	325,000	8,202	34,361	270,239	1,580,453
6	52	2022	65,000.01	65,000.01	390,000	9,284	43,645	350,925	1,605,904
7	53	2023	65,000.01	65,000.01	455,000	10,621	54,266	435,898	1,634,090
8	54	2024	65,000.01	65,000.01	520,000	12,300	66,566	525,723	1,665,699
10 56 2026			**65,000.01**	**65,000.01**	**650,000**	**17,480**	**98,525**	**722,733**	**1,743,920**
11	57	2027	0.00	0.00	650,000	15,918	114,443	761,217	1,781,166
12	58	2028	0.00	0.00	650,000	17,091	131,533	801,712	1,819,964
13	59	2029	0.00	0.00	650,000	18,339	149,873	844,475	1,860,365
14	60	2030	0.00	0.00	650,000	19,744	169,617	889,688	1,902,588
15	61	2031	0.00	0.00	650,000	21,192	190,809	937,326	1,946,598
16	62	2032	0.00	0.00	650,000	22,756	213,565	987,451	1,992,516
17	63	2033	0.00	0.00	650,000	24,419	237,983	1,040,044	2,040,422
18	64	2034	0.00	0.00	650,000	26,155	264,139	1,095,132	2,090,346
19	65	2035	0.00	0.00	650,000	27,938	292,077	1,152,837	2,142,262

DISTRIBUTION PHASE

End of Yr Dur	Age	Year	Annualized Premium Outlay	Cumulative Premium Outlay	Total Dividend	Cumulative Dividends	Cash Surrender Value	Net Death Benefit
20	66	2036	-80,000.00	570,000	29,820	321,896	1,129,588	2,112,559
21	67	2037	-80,000.00	490,000	31,768	353,664	1,105,426	2,081,072
22	68	2038	-80,000.00	410,000	33,808	387,472	1,080,398	2,047,664
23	69	2039	-80,000.00	330,000	35,943	423,415	1,054,458	2,012,193
24	70	2040	-80,000.00	250,000	38,154	461,569	1,027,633	1,974,466
25	71	2041	-80,000.00	170,000	40,563	502,132	999,753	1,934,487
27	73	2043	-80,000.00	10,000	45,971	591,264	940,219	1,847,670
29	75	2045	-80,000.00	-150,000	52,236	692,474	874,661	1,751,560
30	76	2046	-80,000.00	-230,000	55,722	748,196	839,777	1,699,962
31	77	2047	-80,000.00	-310,000	59,464	807,660	803,499	1,645,945
32	78	2048	-80,000.00	-390,000	63,388	871,048	765,503	1,589,360
33	79	2049	-80,000.00	-470,000	67,462	938,510	725,369	1,530,007
34	80	2050	-80,000.00	-550,000	71,767	1,010,277	682,714	1,467,793
35	81	2051	-80,000.00	-630,000	76,155	1,086,432	637,192	1,402,416
36	82	2052	-80,000.00	-710,000	80,695	1,167,127	588,331	1,333,664
37	83	2053	-80,000.00	-790,000	85,351	1,252,478	536,058	1,261,259
38	84	2054	-80,000.00	-870,000	90,134	1,342,612	480,169	1,184,921
39	85	2055	-80,000.00	-950,000	95,093	1,437,705	420,239	1,104,422
40	86	2056	-80,000.00	-1,030,000	100,264	1,537,969	355,726	1,019,574

TAPPING INTO LIFE INSURANCE DIVIDENDS:

It takes time but it's so worth it!

At 65 → $80,000/Yr. 100% tax exempt

Exempt from:
- Federal tax
- State tax
- Local tax
- Medicare premium cancellation
- Provisional income for Social Security taxation

No 1099!

DOLLAR MULTIPLE RETURNS: THE FAMILY GROWTH FACTOR

@ age 73 remaining basis of $10,000

Death benefit of $1,847,670

That is **$184.76 for every $1** of basis

@ age 86 remaining basis of NEGATIVE $1,030,000

Death benefit of $1,019,547

- Took over a million **beyond** basis

- Left over a million for family

Is one "BAD YEAR" worth it for all of that?

Chapter 3
Favorable Tax Treatment of Inside Buildup
Encourages Investment-Oriented Products

Borrowing Against Inside Buildup Is Tax-Free for Life Insurance but Taxable With a Penalty for Annuities

1.

2.

If a policyholder borrows the inside buildup from his or her life insurance policy, the amount borrowed is considered a transfer of capital, not a realization of income, and, therefore, is not subject to taxation. This reasoning is in accord with tax policy on other types of loans, such as consumer loans or home mortgages. These loans are merely transfers of capital or savings from one person to another through a financial intermediary. The ability to borrow against a life insurance policy means that the interest income that is supposed to be building up to fund death benefits can instead be a source of untaxed current income. If the loans are not repaid, the inside buildup will never be taxed; death benefits will simply be reduced by the amount of the loan. Thus, policyholders have the use of tax-free income for purposes other than insurance at the expense of reduced death benefits for their beneficiaries.[5]

The 1982 Tax Equity and Fiscal Responsibility Act treats a loan from an annuity as a distribution of annuity proceeds for tax purposes. The amount borrowed is considered a distribution of interest income first and is subject to tax. The purpose of this treatment is to discourage the use of annuities for short-term investment and tax deferral purposes, while maintaining the tax benefits for long-term investment and retirement uses. Taxing amounts borrowed reduces the incentive to realize income on a current basis from what is meant to be deferred compensation or savings for retirement. If the annuitant has not yet reached the age of 59-1/2 or fulfilled certain other conditions, a penalty tax of 10 percent is also assessed on the amount distributed. Due to the time value of money, it always pays to postpone paying a tax rather than to pay it currently, unless there is some expectation of a significant increase in tax rates in the future. As a result, a penalty is imposed to offset the benefits of deferring the tax on interest income.

Taxation of Policyholder Dividends Paid on Life Insurance Differs From That of Dividends Paid on Annuities

Both life insurance and annuities can pay dividends to policyholders to the extent that investment performance is better than a stated or guaranteed rate of return or to the extent that mortality experience turns out to be better than expected. Part of the investment income on life insurance policies and annuities can be guaranteed, much like a bond or some savings accounts, while part of the investment income can depend on performance and is paid at the discretion of the company, as in certain money market or equity instruments. Investment income paid at the

[5]Similarly, homeowners may borrow against the untaxed equity appreciation in their homes and not pay an income tax on the funds received. However, the interest paid on a home equity loan is tax-deductible, while the interest paid on a life insurance policy loan is not tax-deductible.

GAO/GGD-90-31 Taxation of Inside Buildup

1. If a policyholder borrows the inside buildup from his or her life insurance policy, the amount borrowed is considered a transfer of capital, not a realization of income, and, therefore, is not subject to taxation.

2. The ability to borrow against a life insurance policy means that the interest income that is supposed to be building up to fund death benefits can instead be a source of untaxed current income. If the loans are not repaid, the inside buildup will never be taxed; death benefits will simply be reduced by the amount of the loan. Thus, policyholders have the use of tax-free income for purposes other than insurance at the expense of reduced death benefits for their beneficiaries.

DISCLAIMER

DISCLOSURE AND ACKNOWLEDGMENT

DEFINITIONS

"Acknowledger" as used herein shall mean book reader and/or visitor to Entity's related websites (see "Entity" defined below).

"Entity" as used herein shall mean SMART Publishing Company and/ or SMART Retirement Corporation, and the predecessors, successors, subsidiaries, and other related companies or organizations of SMART Publishing Company and/or SMART Retirement Corporation, and its employees.

TERMS AND CONDITIONS

All of the ideas and opinions expressed are the Entity's. The content within does not constitute and is not meant to serve as individual financial advice. Nor shall any of the content presented be considered tax, legal, planning, investment, or accounting advice. This type of service or advice shall only be given by a professional advisor obtained by the Acknowledger who can review the Acknowledger's current and past financial situations as well as assess future goals. The information contained in this book is not an investment advisory service, is not to be construed as being communicated by an investment advisor, and is provided in a general sense as compared to being customized or personalized under any specific set of facts.

While all facts and numbers have been backed up with sources, the Entity makes no warranty with respect to accuracy. The Entity and publisher assume no responsibility for errors and omissions or for any liability, loss, or damages that occur as a result of reading or using the strategies discussed within this book. No guarantees are made to the Acknowledger regarding the performance of various investment and insurance products, and all illustrations are hypothetical—provided for education purposes only, not to solicit sales or make any guarantees, and shall not be considered investment, tax, accounting, or legal advice. This information shall not be solely relied upon for the purposes of transacting any investment or purchase.

While the concepts discussed may be appropriate for some individuals, the laws of various states and the rules of various insurers and tax authorities should be considered by the Acknowledger and their advisor. While every reasonable attempt has been made to provide accurate content, changes in tax rulings, legislation, and regulations may impact the accuracy of the information and numbers presented.

Your use of the information contained herein is at your own risk. The content is provided "as is" and without warranties of any kind, either expressed or implied. The Entity disclaims all warranties, including, but not limited to, any implied warranties of merchantability, fitness for a particular purpose, title, or noninfringement. The Entity does not promise or guarantee any particular result from your use of the information contained herein. The Entity assumes no liability or responsibility for errors or omissions in the information contained herein.

The Entity will not be liable for any incidental, direct, indirect, punitive, actual, consequential, special, exemplary, or other damages, including, but not limited to, loss or revenue or income, pain and suffering, emotional distress, or similar damages.

Under no circumstances will the Entity be liable for any loss or damage caused by your reliance on the information contained herein. It is your responsibility to evaluate the accuracy, completeness, or usefulness of any information, opinion, advice, or other content contained herein. You are advised to seek the advice of professionals, as appropriate, regarding the evaluation of any specific information, opinion, advice, or other content.

While the illustrations used in this book represent a real, underlying policy, they are still hypothetical and not a guarantee of performance of any individual insurance product. While the company discussed has a strong history of making dividend payment, Acknowledgers should understand that dividends are not guaranteed. Likewise, the amount of a dividend payment is not guaranteed. Acknowledger(s) must work with their own qualified insurance professional and review individual policy documents to fully understand what they may, and may not, receive should they choose to purchase a policy.

Acknowledger affirms that it understands that any data or information entered into calculators or other online tools available to the Entity's website users is subject to redisclosure and may be disseminated by the Entity to its advisors without notice to Acknowledger.

As discussed, in order for policy loans to be tax-free, policies must not become a modified endowment contract (MEC). Should a policy become a MEC, as described by federal tax law, any withdrawals or policy loans may be taxable.

Life insurance policies, including those mentioned in this book, require underwriting to ensure overall insurability of the applicant. The Entity makes no guarantee that the Acknowledger will or can qualify for life insurance. The Entity also makes no representation that policy terms, benefits, cash values, and premiums will be the same or similar to those presented in the book.

The Acknowledger affirms that any sales presentations, tax-aware strategies, and/or planning concepts that may have been provided by the Entity, its employees, and/or representatives demonstrating potential benefits of the plan, should not be relied upon as tax or retirement planning advice regarding the application of the tax laws, now or in the future, to the transaction.

The Acknowledger realizes that any benefits that may be available following the implementation of the plan may be modified by future legislation or changes in the law, or by the insurance company providing the policy.

The Acknowledger represents and warrants to the Entity that the Acknowledger has determined to adopt the plan or purchase the policy only after seeking the advice of independent counsel concerning the tax consequences of the Acknowledger's adoption of the plan or purchase of policy(ies), and that the Acknowledger has not relied upon the Entity with respect to any tax advice concerning the plan or policy.

The Acknowledger also agrees that any disputes that may arise between the Acknowledger and Entity concerning the plan are subject to mandatory arbitration under the auspices of the American Arbitration Association or another arbitration panel mutually agreed upon by the parties. Such arbitration shall be held in the State of West Virginia. The Acknowledger and the Entity will each bear its own attorney fees and costs and shall pay one-half of the arbitrator's fee.